Kinminity

– through the ages

Hugh Cochran

Typeset by W Bailey

Illustrations ©2008 Agata Dymus - Kazmierczak

Printed by F Crowe & Sons Ltd., Norwich

Published by Pica Design, Aboyne, Aberdeenshire

Additional copies of this book can be obtained from
h.cochran@btinternet.com

ISBN 978-0-9561126-1-3

Introduction and Acknowledgements

Kinminity has been part of my family's possessions since my great great grand father Francis James Cochran bought it along with the neighbouring estate of Balfour in 1840. It rather lost its identity then because it became just part of the new combined estate of Balfour, but prior to that, since at least 1170 it had been a separate township of the Parish of Birse.

My interest in it was only kindled after my retirement from legal practice in 1998 when I had enrolled for a course in archaeology and Scottish Studies at Aberdeen University. I became aware that local history and archaeology are very much bound up with each other and that both are becoming more and more topics of public interest. During my course I have had occasion to do an assignment on Craigs Cottage and a dissertation on Kinminity, but both were comparatively short works and I realised that there was a large amount of material I was not using.

When I was considering how to do a larger work, a wise friend said to me "Start with what you've got." I knew I must have a lot of material in a black legal box in the office. And so I had. Old letters, old leases, old title deeds, including a pre-1840 inventory and Francis James Cochran's note book from 1840 all came to light and have been used for the period since 1684. Then I came across the current booming interest in family history. The 1667 Valuation Roll and the 1696 List Of Pollable Persons combined with the inventory of title deeds yielded gold nuggets of information.

My archaeological studies helped me in carrying out the field walk at Birse Kirk and in appraising the cottage at Craigs. My legal background helped in making some sense of the inventory of titles for 18th century Kinminity. However, I did not have sufficient material to enable me to make real sense of the 17th century titles which would have let me see exactly how the tenants of Kinminity actually obtained their first title of ownership after the Reformation. Divine intervention is one possibility, because all titles were complete by about 1700, without any visible links in title.

In writing this story, I have tried to relate what was going on at Kinminity to national events: the coming of Christianity, the triumph of the Gaelic Kingdom of Kenneth McAlpine over the Picts, the defeat of MacBeth by Malcolm Canmore, the gift of Kinminity by King William the Lion to the Bishop of Aberdeen, the Wars of Independence, the lawless behaviour of the caterans in the 14th century, the Reformation, the wars that followed that, the agricultural revolution, the ascendancy of Calvinism in the early 18th century and the arrival of the railway in the 19th century. These events had consequences for the people of Kinminity. What happened to the people and the farm can be seen as a microcosm of the events which happened to people of Scotland over the last two thousand years. In a sense, the 20th century is too close for us to be able to spot trends, but some things are sure. Kinminity is still there, is still beautiful, is still lived in and is still loved.

I hope that this brief account of a long history will be of interest not only to students of Local and Scottish history, but also to those many people who nowadays are trying to trace their own family histories through Family History Societies and on the internet. People with known links to Birse might find the very nugget of information they are looking for. I hope so.

Finally I thank all those who have been supportive in my labours. The book could not have been written save in the context of Robin Callander's book "History in Birse" (2000) and his paper "The Traditional Routes of Birse Parish" (2003). These are both works of great detail and interest, but whereas he has been dealing with the whole Parish, I have had the luxury of being able to enlarge on topics which affect only Kinminity in one way or another. The Parish of Birse is fortunate to have such high quality works of reference available to it. On top of that, Robin has been generous with his time in discussing questions which threatened to baffle me.

I must also thank Anne Harper for much information willingly shared, Norman Newton, one of my Tutors at Aberdeen University, for implanting the idea of doing this publication at all and my wife Beverly for her consistent encouragement and severe editing.

Hugh Cochran   January 2009.

Contents

Photographs, and Maps

Illustrations by Agata Dymus-Kazmierczak

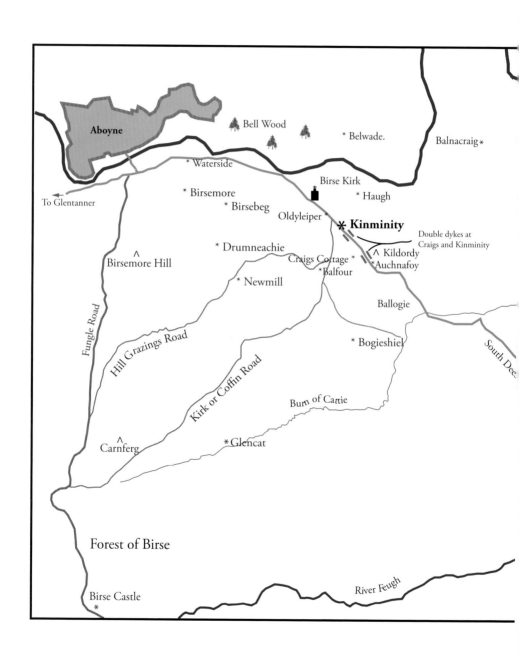

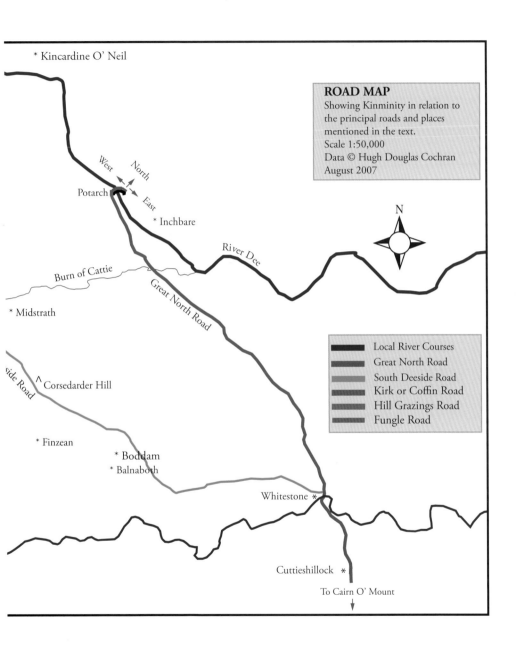

* Kincardine O' Neil

West North

Potarch

East

* Inchbare

River Dee

Burn of Cattie

Great North Road

* Midstrath

side Road

^ Corsedarder Hill

* Finzean

* Boddam
* Balnaboth

Whitestone *

Cuttieshillock *

To Cairn O' Mount

ROAD MAP
Showing Kinminity in relation to
the principal roads and places
mentioned in the text.
Scale 1:50,000
Data © Hugh Douglas Cochran
August 2007

N

Local River Courses
Great North Road
South Deeside Road
Kirk or Coffin Road
Hill Grazings Road
Fungle Road

Chapter 1
An Overview

There is an unusual amount of information available about this small corner of the Parish of Birse just south of the River Dee about a mile east of Aboyne in Aberdeenshire. The Road Map can be used as a location plan to identify the places named in this book . A copy of part of David Walker's Map of 1840 is on page 58 which shows how the "Tounship" of Kinminity and the field layout would have looked in the 18th Century. One other map from William Roy is reproduced on page 26 and on the cover and these maps are referred to when relevant. This work will trace the history of the ground from the earliest known period of human habitation in Neolithic times, through the Iron Age and Pictish times and the coming of Christianity to the time when Scotland was dominated by the Gaelic speaking Scots. In each of these periods we have a tiny glimpse of what was happening in Birse. We will then move on to the historic period from which documentary evidence survives. Charters granted by a Pope and a King demonstrate that Birse was a parish in the twelfth Century and of sufficient importance to be gifted by the King to the Bishop of Aberdeen whose successors held it to the exclusion of all lay barons for very nearly four hundred years. However the collapse of the Diocese of Aberdeen at the Reformation brought sweeping changes. A power vacuum followed when all Church land in Scotland seemed to be up for grabs by local Barons great and small. Birse was no exception, but one small farm, Kinminity, was different. Here the four tenants somehow managed to hold on to their shares of the land and by the middle of the seventeenth century we find titles in the names of the former tenant families. This farm was not in single ownership until the year 1803. Indeed it is likely that one of the families by the name of Turner who owned a share of Kinminity in 1760 was of the same family as the Turners who were tenants of the Diocese in 1511.

In the 18th century we are fortunate to have access to many of the minutes of the Kirk Session during the period when the Calvinist Church of Scotland was still following its policy of public discipline and nearly all the cases brought before it were for "unclean fornication". No case involving anyone from Kinminity has been found, but some very close neighbours appear in their pages. Then in 1792 we have the first of three Statistical Accounts, which all give us an account of what was actually happening in Birse in the years they were written. From a previously unseen source, we also have some unexpected insight into the character of the author of the 1792 Account, the Reverend Joseph Smith. From the same source and with a bit of detective work we learn about Cutty Sievewright who built the now ruined cottage of Craigs, just a field away from Kinminity itself. These two characters bring the 18th century alive for us in a way that no statistics or title deeds could possibly do.

The 18th and 19th centuries brought great changes to an agricultural holding like Kinminity. Lime brought new productivity to the land, but with the ownership split between different owners, runn-rigg farming continued and efficiency was lost.   It was no longer possible for up to four separate owners sharing the township of twenty two separate structures for either men or animals, to go on farming in the same way as before. In 1803 the Earl of Aboyne bought the whole of Kinminity from the different owners and between 1840 and 1857 the next owner demolished the medieval cluster of buildings that formed the Township and erected the steading and perhaps also the farmhouse that stand there today. In the 21st century, the steading has been converted for use as two dwelling houses.

Chapter 2
The Site

The site we are considering is Kinminity, but it cannot be considered in isolation. We have to look at the places nearby and these are mainly sited along the road coloured green on the Roadmap in the introductory pages of this book. Other places not on the green road will feature and the intention is that all such places as are mentioned in the text are also shown on the Roadmap if at all possible.

The South Deeside Road, coloured green stretches from south of the Dee at Aboyne and goes past Birse Church, through Kinminity, over the hill at Craigs Cottage and onwards to Whitestone where it joins the Great North Road which goes over the Cairn o'Mount and on to the South. Callander (2003) considers this road to be as ancient as the Cairn o'Mount and Fungle roads, although the precise route it has followed has changed over the centuries.

Joining the South Deeside Road at Oldyleiper is the Church or Coffin Road coloured mauve which forks to go left to mid Glencat or straight on to Upper Feughside and the Forest of Birse. The lines of communication affecting Kinminity are more fully dealt with in Chapter 13 but for the moment it is enough if we become familiar with the outlines of the area we will be looking at later in detail.

It is also worth having a look at the meanings of some of the place names in our site:-

Birse   The name is probably as old as the original church possibly founded in the 5th century . If so, it would have roots in the language spoken by the Picts. In the historical period, it appears in various forms namely Brass, Bras, Birs and Praes. Macdonald (1899:59) says that the common derivation from Praes, a bush, is extremely doubtful and Browne (1923:185) agrees, saying that the meaning is entirely lost.

Kinminity   This is Gaelic and therefore must date from after the mid ninth century when Kenneth McAlpine destroyed the Pictish kingdoms in Scotland unifying the land under his Gaelic speaking Scots. The name appears in documents as Kinmonty, Kinmonedy, Kinmaunity and Kinmonety. All sources agree it comes from the Gaelic *Caenn monaidh* meaning "Muir head" or "Muir end" but Dinnie (1865:63) suggests "Top of the mount".

Kildordy   Nicholaisen (2001:166) says that names beginning with the Gaelic *Kil-* often point to a background of the presence of churches, churchyards or hermit's cells, but not always. Sometimes, and particularly in North East Scotland, the *Kil-* is a corrupt form of *coille* (wood) or *cull* (nook). The -dordy is probably a personal name and one candidate is Dardanus, a local Pictish king to whom there is a stone in memory at the top of the nearby hill crossing at Corsedardar (Aberdeenshire SMR Site ref NO59SE0003). It is not unusual to find a Pictish place name with a Gaelic prefix.

Glencat   Both Browne (1923:186) and Macdonald (1899:203) give - "the glen of the wild cat", from *Gleann Cait*.

Balfour   *Bal-* just means township or place and Browne (1923:185) and Macdonald (1899:42) quote *Baile fuar* to mean either "cold place" or "place of the pasture land", from the Welsh (and therefore probably Pictish) word *pawr*, but Nicholaisen sees only the Gaelic *por* (pasture) , or Welsh *pawr* there.

Balnaboth   Browne (1923:185) and Macdonald (1899:46) agree on *Baile nam both* - "the town of the huts or bothies".

Finzean   Browne (1923:186) and Macdonald (1899:188) agree again on *Fionn-an*, meaning "a fair or light coloured place".

Aboyne   Only Macdonald (1899:3) hazards an opinion here. After giving the various alternative spellings (Obein, Obeyn, Obyn, Aboyn), he surmises that it may be a personal name or part of a personal name (cf Kincardine o'Neil) and compares the Irish Taghboyne and Ennisboyne which are derived from the personal name *Baeithin*

Auchnafoy   Macdonald (1899:32) gives *Achadh na faiche* meaning "the field of the exercise green"

Drumneachy   Browne (1923) gives *Druim an atha*, "the ridge of the ford".

River Dee   The northern boundary of the parish near Birse Kirk is the river Dee. Nicholaisen (2001:229) argues that a sizeable number of names of natural features including river names survive from very early or pre-Celtic times, including the name of the river Dee. He puts this down to the important roles water courses have always played as life sustaining sources of water and of fertile alluvial soil, as means of communication, as obstacles, as boundaries, as objects of religious worship and that for these reasons the names tend to survive changes of culture and of language.   In the case of the Dee, he sees the Celtic word *Deu-* meaning god or divine person as the root, with the addition of a suffix -a to make *Deu-a*. Ptolemy calls the Dee the *Deva* which shows that the Roman explorers and mapmakers were hearing the same sound and Nicholaisen compares that to *Deu-ona* which with a different suffix became the river Don.

The Church

Fig. 2.1 The so called Crusaders Stone now in Birse Church. (Photo by W. Bailey. ABIPP)

Aberdeenshire SMR (Ref NO59NE0017) record that there are no remains of the Medieval Church. In the present church like in so many Presbyterian Churches of that period, the pulpit was at first high up on the south wall with the congregation facing the minister. This was to escape from what was considered the Popish traditional east/west orientation of having the altar at the east end. It also enhanced the perceived importance of the sermon (the word) over the traditional Mass. Two other local churches still have the pulpit on the south wall, namely Aboyne and Glen Buchat churches.

A 14th -15th Century sculptured stone which was discovered in the foundations in 1779 was built in to the outside wall of the churchyard, but rests now within the Church in the room immediately to the left on entry and is shown opposite. The decoration represents a sword and two small crosses. Renovations took place in 1933 which restored the east/west orientation of the Church and saw three windows inserted in the north wall and the pulpit, communion table and font all relocated at the east end. This makes it a light and spacious building internally, but externally it is still of typical 18th Century Scottish Presbyterian design. Today it no longer serves as a church, but is under the governance of a Charitable Trust which makes it available for use by the local community.

Other features close to our site

To the north of Birse Kirk is the Belwood Boat near where the Tarland Burn joins the River Dee from the north. This is mentioned by Browne (1923 : 218) where a fourth part of the title to the Boat was conveyed by Charter in 1591 by the Earl of Aboyne to Robert Davidson. Browne tells us that the crossing was directly opposite to the Kirk at Birse and was exceedingly dangerous.

About a mile to the north of the crossing lies the medieval church of Formaston, shown also in the records as Aboyne Church and we can presume that early communication between the two churches was by this crossing.

Proceeding south-east through Kinminity, the road crosses the hill between Craigs Cottage and Kildordy where an enclosure (probably military) can just be seen. Other nearby features are crop marks of three Iron Age souterrains and the site of a timber hut stance in the field immediately to the north of the walled garden at Balfour mansion house (Aberdeenshire SMR Site ref NO59NE0044). The remains of a possible medieval tower can be seen in the wood to the south of Mains of Balfour (Aberdeenshire SMR ref NO59NE0053). As we shall see, the whole of the parish of Birse belonged to the Diocese of Aberdeen in the Medieval period, so it is possible that this was a hunting lodge of the Bishop, like the lodge at Easter Clune, Finzean.

Chapter 3

From pre-history to the Middle Ages

Neolithic/Bronze Age.
Very little survives from this period, but a field walking exercise took place on 22nd March 1998 in the field immediately north of Birse Church and the report of that exercise including a site plan is reproduced in the Appendix. A flint knife and a flint arrowhead were found which are enough to confirm the presence of prehistoric man very near to the Church site.

Iron Age / Pictish period.
The souterrains near Balfour Mansion House have already been referred to. There is also a fragment of a Pictish Class 1 symbol stone built in to the garden wall of the Manse by the Church, (Aberdeenshire SMR Site ref

Fig. 3.1 The Class I Pictish Symbol Stone in the Manse Garden

NO59NE0052). A photo is reproduced as Fig. 3.1. The stone measures roughly 30cm square and bears the almost complete incised symbol of a double sided comb. While this is only circumstantial evidence of a Pictish presence, (the stone could have been transported from elsewhere to build the wall), it is wholly consistent with St Colm's foundation of the church there in the 5th Century.

Early Christianity.

Wyness (1968:22) records that Christianity came to Deeside in waves from three sources - the first came early in the 5th century, from St Ninian's monastery at Whithorn; the second a century later from St Moluag's establishment at Bangor in N. Ireland and the third during the 7th century from St Kentigern's foundation in Glasgow. He tells us that Birse was evangelised in the first of these waves by St Colm, a follower of St Ninian, who lived about 400 AD just about the time of the end of the Roman occupation of Britain. Wyness tells us that St Colm is said to have *"established a church at Birse, but his activities in that district were somewhat obscure through the church of Rome later replacing him by St Michael, to whom the Kirk of Birse was dedicated. On Gannoch Hill is the site of St Colm's Well - once a place of pilgrimage on the Saint's Feast day, 16th October"*. St Colm's Well is marked on the modern O.S. Map at Ref NO 494 881 near the top of the Firmounth Pass between Edzell and Dinnet. This is all well within the Pictish period and if our surmise is right that there was a Pictish settlement at Birse that makes it an obvious place for St Colm to go to found his church.

The Malcolm Legend I.

Dinnie (1865:64) tells this tale in these words:- *"According to tradition, the first of the family in Kinminity who took the name of Malcolm was tenant in the reign of Malcolm Canmore. Happening to be at some of the wars with the King, who, in some way not related, lost his horse which ran off, this man fetching the horse again and bringing it to the King, was rewarded with a grant to him and his heirs for ever, of whatever lands he possessed on lease of Kinminity at the time"*.

Illus. 1. St Colm brings Christianity to the Picts at Birse in the early 5th Century.

Illus. 2. The gift of the Parish of Birse by King William the Lion in 1170.

Dinnie goes on to explain that this first charter is said to have been written on the bark of a birch tree. There was certainly a family of Malcolms in possession at Kinminity from 1667 to 1857, but there is no evidence to support or refute the legend prior to 1667. We will revert to this topic in Chap. 6

Confirmation of grant of Birse Church by the Pope to the Bishop of Aberdeen.

In 1157 Pope Adrian IV, the only English Pope, signed a document which bears to be in confirmation of previous grants to the Bishops of Aberdeen by Kings and Princes. The document is dated at Segnia (Segni) but as Browne (1923:187) points out the subjects confirmed are restricted to *"the church of Brass with its pertinents"*. No mention of the Parish, nor even of the "vill of the church".

The gift of the Parish by the King to Mathew, Bishop of the Diocese of Aberdeen and his successors.

It was not until a few years later in 1170 that William the Lion, *"Willelmus Dei gratia rex Scotorum"* granted to Mathew, Bishop of Aberdeen and his successors a deed in increment of his possessions in the following terms:-
"--- hac carta mea confermavi de incremento predicto episcopo Matheo et successoribus suis ---- totas terras meas de Brass videlicet --- Ochtirbrass, Drummenathy, villam ecclesie, Kynmonedy, Balfoure -- (here are enumerated 12 other holdings in Birse) -- *et forestam meam de Brass cum omnibus nativis dictarum terrarum, thaynis meis tantum exclusis."* (Registrum Vol I:12)

So by this deed the Bishops of Aberdeen fell heirs to not only the church building itself and its pertinents, but also all the named holdings in the parish, including Kinminity and the forests. The deed of 1157 included only the church and its pertinents. The 1170 deed included the *villam ecclesie*, the vill of the church, or Kirkton as we would now say.

The last words *"with all the natives of the said lands my thaynes only excepted"* are worth a comment as there must be some uncertainty about what they mean. To include the "natives" probably meant that the feudal obligations of the tenantry were transferred from obligations directly to the king to obligations to the Bishop. But what of the exclusion of the "thaynes"? Thanes, in Scotland, according to The Century Dictionary (1899), were a class of non-military tenants of the crown and the title was in use till the end of the 15th century. We know of no thanes in Birse and the term may be no more than a "catch all" phrase put into all grants of land by the King. Let us suppose however that the alleged grant of land by Malcolm Canmore to Malcolm of Kinminity (written on the bark of a birch tree) raised him to the status of a thane. His land would in those circumstances be excluded from the grant by King William the Lion to the Bishop. Again, we will come back to this intriguing possibility.

But we must also ask the question, Why did King William make this gift? The most likely answer is that he did it to enhance his chances of going to Heaven. This was the age of unequalled expansion of the Monastic Orders, when Kings, Barons and anyone with money gave land and resources to the Orders to build a monastery, on the condition that the Monks prayed in perpetuity for the soul of the donor. Giving land to the Church is likely to have been on the same terms. King William, by the Grace of God, King of the Scots, then in the fifth year of his forty-nine year reign would have wanted to fulfil pledges by previous Kings and Princes to make this gift and also to get the credit for having done so. Another of his benefactions was the foundation of Arbroath Abbey where the famous Declaration of Arbroath was signed in 1320. The motivation for these acts of largesse on the part of Kings and Barons can be argued about, but there is no doubt that to create stable institutions like Monasteries and Dioceses loyal to the King helped him to create stable government.

Historians do not have very much good to say about King William who spent five months in 1174 in a dungeon in Falaise, Normandy as a prisoner of Henry II of England. The south of Scotland was occupied by English garrisons, at Scottish expense. Even if the occupants of Kinminity did not hear about their King's capture at the time they would have heard about it when it came to paying for the English presence. As for his soubriquet "The Lion" there are three theories. He was the first Scottish king to adopt the Lion Rampant on his coat of arms, it was because of his "rough and stern countenance" and because John of Fordun, a 14th century chronicler referred to him as *"leo justitiae"* , a lion of justice. (Magnusson 2001: 86) The tenants at Kinminity would not have had to bother about that, because apparently he was never called "The Lion" in his lifetime. It was because of him however that Kinminity was held as a tenancy of the Diocese of Aberdeen for the next 400 years.

The Languages spoken in Birse in 1170.

About three hundred years have now passed since Kenneth McAlpine destroyed the Pictish culture and language and Gaelic became the predominant language of the people. This is clear from the large number of place names in Birse with Gaelic roots. We only need to look at the names in the Charter of 1170. The three names quoted , Ouchtirbrass, *(uachdar-brass)* Drumenathy, *(druim an atha)* and Balfoure *(baile fuar)* all have obvious Gaelic roots but already by 1170 the spelling is corrupt. This was due to the steadily increasing English influence in Scotland. About a century before, in 1057, Malcolm Canmore had defeated the last truly Celtic King of Scotland, Macbeth and Malcolm's Saxon wife the Saint Queen Margaret opened up Scotland to English influences. Up the East Coast a dialect of the pre-Chaucerian English language became the vernacular, and by 1170 this was creeping inland as far as Birse. The changed spelling of the place names confirms this. While the language of the Church and the Law was Latin, the drafter of the Charter had to use the place names as spoken by the people and we can already see a shift away from Gaelic spelling at this date. Could the tenants at Kinminity already be speaking in an early Aberdeenshire Doric dialect?
Languages are deliberately referred to in the plural in this section, (Gaelic and English) for it is thought that Gaelic was understood right up to the end of the 18th century in the upper reaches of the Forest of Birse (First Statistical Account 1792:18) and even later in some of the remoter glens

of Upper Deeside. The two languages will have co-existed side by side for a long time, but the names of the tenants in the 1511 Rental (see below) show an English bias. Names like Anderson, Turner, Harper and Robertson predominate, and there are no Mac's. Ross and Rose look like the only possible Gaelic names.

The Rental of the Bishopric of Aberdeen, 1511.

Our next glimpse of Kinminity in the written records is the Rental of 1511 (Registrum Vol I:372). Presumably the Diocese collected rent every year from its tenants, but only one rental statement survives, that of 1511. So far as money is concerned, the total rental is £699. 7s. 8d., of which the parish of Brass produces £147. 5s. 8d. The entry for Kinminity is:-

> *Kynmonedy ij aratra . gressuma v lib . vi. s. viij. d.*
> *Assedatur . pro .vj .lib in anno , una marta, ij mutonibus,*
> *ij . Aucis , vj . gallinis, j.b. avenarum cum pobulo ,*
> *iij.s.iiij.d pro bondagio , j. b . victual et vj oneribus lignorum.*
> *Johanni Turnour vj b   Malcolm Willelmi iiij b*
> *Thome Durvart ij b   Johanni Turnour juniori   iiij b*

which Browne (1923:193) translates into English:-

> Kynmonty . Two ploughs. Entry fee £5 6s 8d.
> Yearly rent £6: 1 mart, 2 mutons, 2 geese, 6 poultry,
> 1 boll oats with fodder, 3s 4d for bondage,
> 1 boll victuals and 6 loads of logs.
> Tenants. John Turnour 6 bovates Malcolm Williams 4 bovates
> Thomas Durvart 2 bovates John Turnour Jun 4 bovates.

But further translation is necessary and Browne (1923: 192) supplies this also. The entry fee, Latin *gressuma*, Scots *grassum,* is the fee payable by a tenant on first entry or renewal of the lease. Marts and Mutons are cattle and sheep in carcase. Victuals are any kind of grain. "With fodder", Latin *cum pobulo,* means with the straw, and bondage is the labour due from the farmer to the lord. Services where due are the labour due from the serfs on the farm to the farmer. In this case the bishop receives the money value of both.

There were a total of 25 separate holdings in the Parish of Birse from which the Bishop collected rent. There are 20 "two plough" holdings and in each case there are 16 bovates, divided in different proportions between the tenants. The explanation is that a team of oxen was eight, so a two plough farm had sixteen bovates or oxen. The Century Dictionary puts it concisely:- "The bovate or oxgang represented the tillage, not of an ox team, but of one of the team, that is, it was the share of the tilled land appropriated to the owner of one of the eight associated oxen contributed to the cooperative eight ox plough". Attempts have been made to relate a bovate or an oxgang to an area of land, but until the next century this is a futile exercise. Some put it as high as 15 acres. Kinminity was a two plough or 16 bovate holding, as were most of the other holdings in Birse. A modern estimate of its acreage then is 131 acres, which would mean that one bovate was 8.1 acres. The land at Kinminity is hilly, so the worse the land, the less area per bovate. The whole system was founded not on how big was the farm, but on how the shares of the produce were divided. The differences between the farms is reflected in the different rents, entry fees and payments in kind.

Chapter 4
The Wars of Independence and the Turbulent 14th Century
and Law and Order in Birse

We have little knowledge about how the Wars of Independence affected Birse and Kinminity. Wyness (1968:60) tells us how on 13th July 1296 Edward I of England crossed the Mounth at the Crynes Corse Pass and arrived at Durris with 30,000 men-at-arms and 5000 mail-clad knights. After receiving the submission and homage of four Deeside Barons and marching to Elgin, Edward returned to Kincardine o'Neil where he forded the Dee and took the Cairn o'Mount route south to the Mearns. Edward came back in August 1303, when after again visiting Elgin, he camped at Kincardine o'Neil and on 17th October travelled south by the Cairn o'Mount. We only have to look at our Roadmap to see how near Kinminity is to Edward's routes south. To feed and sustain an army of 35,000 men needs an immense amount of supplies and we can guess that some of those supplies came from Kinminity.

Winning the battle of Bannockburn in 1314 did not end the Wars of Independence for Scotland. Those Barons who in Scotland and on Deeside had paid homage to Edward lost their lands and their families became known as the Dispossessed. They carried on the fight. One of these was Earl David of Strathbogie, a descendant of the Comyn family who lost the Earldom of Buchan in the Wars through siding with King Edward. This resulted in a battle on the slopes of Morven, some ten miles from and within sight of Kinminity in 1335, where Earl David was defeated by Sir Andrew de Moray at Culblean. This battle is now considered to be the last and decisive battle of the Wars of Independence when the Dispossessed, who hankered for the King of England to return and restore their lands and titles to them, were finally vanquished.

The 14th century was a turbulent and unstable period, comparing badly with the prosperous and more peaceful 13th century in Scotland. Not only was there the Black Death which ravaged Scotland and the whole of Europe (of which we hear nothing in Kinminity or Birse), but there was the continuing ethnic conflict between the Gaelic and the English speaking populations which culminated in the Battle of Harlaw in 1411. Birse and Kinminity were on the front line between these two cultures.

The following account of 14th century events, as they did or may have affected Kinminity, is an amalgam of the various documents and comments reproduced in The Records of Aboyne (1894:91-92) and Browne (1923:189-192), with the writer's own interpretation of those accounts.

It was difficult for the Scottish King to control the remoter parts of Scotland from the South and so he adopted a policy of installing "Strong Men" in those areas. The problem in the north was the menace of the Caterans. These were groups of Gaelic speaking brigands who ran protection rackets. Either the local farmers supplied them with food and sustenance or their property would be mysteriously burnt down. The "Strong Man" appointed by King Robert II (1370-90) to govern and control the North of Scotland was his younger and favourite son, Alexander Stewart, more commonly known as The Wolf of Badenoch. It is not our remit to discuss his dispute with the Bishop of Moray resulting in the fire at Elgin Cathedral except to say that the Wolf was himself much criticised at the time for using Caterans to obtain his own allegedly lawful ends. Rather we will deal with the complaint made by Bishop Adam of Aberdeen to the King that the Grants and the Mackintoshes had more than once lifted the "merts" (cattle) and "muttons" (sheep) of Deeside and retired to the shelter of the Forest of Birse where many a deadly conflict took place between the caterans and the raided tenants. The substance of the complaint was that *"Ferchard M'yntoshy , by himself and his agents brought great loss upon the church lands and the inhabitants of Birse, daily afflicting them with such threats and terrors that they could not and dared not remain in their dwellings and cultivate their land and could not , by reason of their fear, live faithful in peace and enjoy their goods"*. In a response dated at Perth on 8th June 1382 the King's Council ordered Alexander and the Sheriff of Inverness to take sufficient surety from

Ferchard that he and his agents should not do any damage, contrary to law, to the bishop's lands or the inhabitants or their goods under pain of loss of life and limb and all that he could lose to King and Council; and intimating to Ferchard that if he wished to prosecute the Bishop in form of law before the King or the Council they would hear him.

This latter *proviso* is seen by some commentators as suggesting that Ferchard and the M'Intoshes had some colourable claim to the lands of Birse, though it is difficult to see how this could be so in the light of the Bishop's unambiguous title of 1170. Nevertheless it could shed some light on the question of how after the Reformation the Farquharsons, thought to be lineal descendants of Ferchard, obtained their title to Finzean.

But to return to the events of 1382, the response of the King's Council was evidently ineffective, because the Bishop of Aberdeen had to appoint a powerful Baron to protect the tenants and their interests and hence the creation of a hereditary Bailie of Birse whose job it was do that. But it was not until over a hundred years later, in 1489 that the Bishop received from the Crown the Free Regality of his lands in Birse (Gilbert 1979: 188). The Century Dictionary (1899) defines "Regality" in Scotland as *"a territorial jurisdiction formerly conferred by the king. The lands over which this jurisdiction extended were said to be given in liberum regalitatem and the persons receiving the right were termed Lords of Regality and exercised the highest prerogatives of the Crown"*. This right included the power of life or death over the inhabitants of the area of jurisdiction in 1489, but before he had actually received the right of Free Regality, the Bishop, William Elphinstone pursued Sir David de Lindesay of Beaufort the current Bailie of Birse, for theft of a long list goods including 12 oxen and 8 cows from the tenants in Birse. Needless to say the Bailie claimed these were his by right by virtue of his capacity of Bailie and for the yearly pension due to him by the Bishop. The Lords Auditors, after deliberation, decreed that Sir David did wrong to steal the goods, but he committed no theft because he did it *"be a colourit richt"*. He must deliver the goods to the Bishop and in time to come desist from exercising his office of Bailie.

In the context of the general law and order of the kingdom, it can be argued that the appointment of Lords of Regality, who were mainly only created north of the Forth, had a stabilising effect on these remote districts. Justice could be exercised more effectively and more quickly. To that extent, the tenants of Kinminity will have felt some protection. Callander (2000:89) narrates how Bishop William set up a centre of administration at Marywell and Midstrath near to the location later known as Gallowhill, where the lime quarry and kiln now are (see Chapter 8). But throughout all this period, the tenants of Kinminity will have seen armies and caterans and Bailies come and go, all of them apparently bent on stealing as much as possible from them. As the Roadmap shows, there are two principal entrances to the Parish of Birse from the north. One was by the Fungle Road, leading to the Forest and the other was right through Kinminity along the South Deeside Road. The tenants there were completely exposed to whoever came along the road. Neither the King, nor his Strong Man the Wolf of Badenoch, nor the Bishop, nor the Bailie of Birse succeeded in affording them much protection from the activities of the caterans and in the 17th century the Courts of Regality themselves became oppressors. There were over a hundred such Courts in Scotland in which the great owners of land presided as hereditary barons or sheriffs, having power to sentence all criminals in their domain, wielding the right of punishment of pit and gallows - to imprison or hang. These courts, which acquired a reputation for committing gross miscarriages of justice, were abolished in 1748, but memories of them were still vivid at the end of that century. No specific tales of injustice have come down to us concerning Kinminity or Birse, but there must have been some hangings, otherwise why would there be two Gallowhills in the Parish? Writing in the 1792 Statistical Account, (p 24) the Reverend Joseph Smith, of whom we shall hear much more in Chapter 10 of this narrative, writes *"To the north-east of Finzean, is a hill called the Gallow Hill. Another is near to Ballogie. There the Barons of old, who held their estates with power of pit and gallows, put to death any of their tenants or dependents, who were so unfortunate as to fall under their displeasure. What blessed days do we now enjoy, in comparison of these? How thankful to God and loyal to the King ought we therefore to be? Our case has*

been meliorated and , by a wise Legislature, will, by degrees be so still".
The appointment of a Bailie, who in Birse stole from the tenants himself
and   the creation of Courts of Regality which later turned into local
kangaroo courts, were two responses by the king to the problem of how
to deal with lawlessness in the land. It can be said of both measures that
the cure was as bad as the disease.

Chapter 5
The Reformation and the collapse of the Diocese

The last great Bishop of Aberdeen was Bishop William Elphinstone who died in 1514 not long after the Battle of Flodden and the compilation of our Rental for the Parish of Birse in 1511. As well as founding the University of Aberdeen, he was a Man of Letters, with international connections and he conceived the idea of building the Bridge of Dee in Aberdeen which was completed in early 1527. He was succeeded after an interim bishop by Bishop Gavin Dunbar (1518-1531) who completed the Bridge and was a good steward of the resources of the Diocese. William Gordon, the last of the pre-Reformation Bishops and fourth son of the Earl of Huntly was bishop from 1546 to 1577. Spottiswood (1655) has this to say of him :- *"He dilapidated the whole rents by feuing the lands and converting the victual duties into money, a great part whereof he wasted upon his base children and the whores, their mothers"* (Records of Aboyne:90)

These dilapidations were not wholesale however. Browne (1923:206) quotes 46 assedations (leases) at Birse in 1549 two of them at Kinminity. The first was a lease dated 13th October 1549 of *"four oxingang of the land and toun of Kynmondy to Thomas Downe"*. The lease was for three years up to nineteen years, at a rent of 33/4d per annum, with similar but not identical payments in kind to those in the 1511 rental. The other Kinminity lease of the same date was of *"four oxingang of land of the toun and Landis of Kynmondy made be the Bishop to Johne Davidsoun for all the termis of Auchtene yeiris"* at the same rent of 33/4d.

We can draw three conclusions from these leases. First that the holding was probably still divided into four parts, each of them of four oxgangs or bovates; second that the obligation to pay the rent and services has shifted from a joint obligation on the four tenants mentioned in the 1511 Rental to an individual obligation in 1549 to pay a quarter of the whole rent on each tenant; and third that the rent has increased slightly. The rent of the whole holding in 1511 was £6. A quarter of that for four ox gangs would

Illus. 3. The Reformation 1560.

be £1-10/-It has gone up to £1-13/4.

It is difficult to know what money was worth in 1549, but we must assume the currency in question to be the pound Scots. Browne (1923:207) quotes from a lease in March 1549 by the Bishop *"to George Erle of Huntlie --*
------ of the baronye and schire of Fetterneir with the place of fisching" For the *"fisching"* he was to pay   *"ane berrall salmond or thre pundis money at the option of the said noble lord"* We also learn from Buchanan's Tables (Edinburgh 1829) that a barrel of salmon was 42 gallons. So the yearly rent of four *"oxingangs"* at Kinminity in 1549 (£1-13/4) would have bought just over 21 gallons (say 23 gallons) of salted salmon.

It was not till later that the "Dilapidations" took effect. For example:-

On 25th June 1558 Bishop William grants a Charter to John Stewart of Balfour adjoining Kinminity for an unspecified price. This Charter is unusual because it contains an obligation on John Stewart *"to maintain and defend as far as he can the Bishop and his successors in the See of Aberdeen, the Dean and Canons of the same, in their persons, goods and lands and also the orthodox Christian faith"* (Records of Aboyne:96). Is the Bishop worrying here about the future course of events?

In 1567 the Bishop's Chancellor, Alexander Settoun   gives the said John Stewart in hereditary fee farm, again for an unspecified price, *"the shadow half of all the lands and churchtoun of Bras -----"* (Records of Aboyne:104), also adjoining Kinminity. The   lands of the Churchtoun will have lain round the Church, which is at about the lowest part of the Parish and the land rises towards the south. The "shadow half" will have been the north facing area around where Mains of Balfour now stands. Other disposals were taking place not only in Birse but of other lands owned by the Diocese.

What was behind this disintegration of the church and of its lands? There were two factors. One was the moral degeneracy of some of the Church figures. On 5th Jan 1559 the Dean and Chapter of Aberdeen petitioned Bishop William Gordon *"That My Lorde of Aberdene cause the kirkmen within his Lordship's Diocie to reforme themselves in all thair slanderous manner of Lyving, and to remove thair oppin concubins, alswels greit as small: and the Cheptoure of Aberdene sall do sicklike amangis thaim in all sharpest maner ...... And the Deyne and Cheptour forsaidis humblie and hartlie prayis and exhortis my lord thair ordinar ---- that his lordschip be so gude as to schew gude and edificative example; in speciale in removing and discharging himself of company of the gentill woman in quhom he is gretlie slanderit"* (Registrum Vol I:41). So the Dean and Chapter were at least making an attempt at reform from within. But it was too late and anyway, Bishop William paid no attention. Six years later in 1565, he granted a Charter of land at North Spittal to Janet Knowles (probably the *"gentill woman in quhom he was gretlie slanderit"*) in liferent, and in fee to George, John, William, Elizabeth, Margaret, and Martha, her six children by the Bishop. (Records of Aboyne 1894:104)

The second factor appeared on a national scale. On 24th August 1560 the Estates in Edinburgh passed three Acts. The first abolished the Pope's authority over the land, and the jurisdiction of all Catholic Prelates. The second annulled all Acts of previous Parliaments supporting the old doctrines. The third forbad the saying or hearing or being present at Mass. The penalties were:- For a first offence, confiscation of goods, for a second offence, banishment, and for a third offence, death. Browne (1923:215) tells us what happened. Superintendents were appointed as overseers of areas roughly corresponding to the Diocese areas. Two thirds of the Church endowments were assigned to the old clergy, and one third was attached by the Crown for the common affairs of the country.

So the tenants at Kinminity suddenly had a new Landlord, The State. However in 1577 the title of Bishop was restored and given to the Superintendents, three of whom in Scotland were the old Bishops who had accepted the new office. They were called Tulchan Bishops. A tulchan was a calf's skin stuffed with straw and set beside a cow to make her give her milk. The name was derisively given to the persons appointed as titular Bishops in Scotland in whose names the revenues were drawn by whoever who had appropriated them. Bishop William Gordon died in 1577 so he lived to see all these changes.

The repercussions of the Reformation rolled on through the 17th and 18th centuries. In the 17th century, more and more names turn up as owners of parts of Birse until there were 21 in 1667. At the same time the Civil War was being played out, and it seems that Kinminity was affected by this too.

The "fort" at Kildordy.

This used to be known in my family as the Roman Camp. Dinnie (1865:66) records that the circular camp on the top of Kildordy Hill is said to have

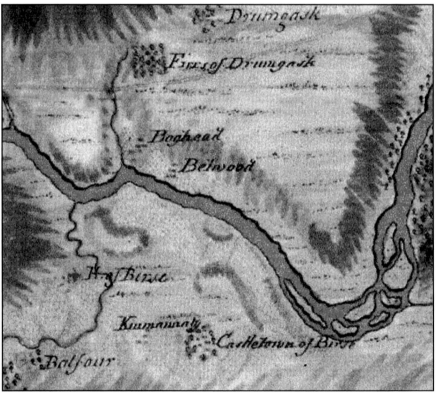

Fig 5.1. Detail from William Roy's "Great Map" showing "Castletown of Birse" where the Kildordy Fort now stands. Reproduced by kind permission of the British Library.

been used by a party of Montrose's soldiers in 1645 under the command of Major M'Donald. Quoting Spalding, he says that *"Montrose directed M'Donald north into Birse, Cromar, and Glentanner, and himself passed south towards Dunkeld"*. There is no evidence that a party of Montrose's

Fig. 5.2.
David Cochran demonstrates the remains of the rampart at Kildordy

soldiers camped here, and Aberdeenshire SMR (Site Ref NO59NE0026) repeats Dinnie's version, but adds " --- *the impression is gained of a prehistoric funerary monument rather than a defensive structure*". However William Roy's map drawn a century later between 1747 and 1755 gives credence to Dinnie's account, and shows "Castletown of Birse" not far East of Kinminity in almost exactly the place where Kildordy is. Now known as "The Great Map", it was nothing short of a detailed military survey of the whole of mainland Scotland, which was to have a great influence on the future of mapping. A very small part of it is reproduced in Fig 5.1. Roy as a military mapmaker for the Hanoverian Army would have been very interested in anything that had the appearance of a defensive site. Very little remains of the "fort" as can be seen from the photograph of David Cochran with one foot on the rampart, (Fig 5.2.)

If Montrose's soldiers did camp there, we may imagine that the tenants at Kinminity fared no better than all civilian populations fared when they were visited by the rude soldiery.

Chapter 6
The Malcolm Legend II

We have seen in Chapter 3 what Dinnie (1865:64) has told us about the gift by King Malcolm to the tenant at Kinminity called Malcolm. He speaks of a battle in which both Malcolms were engaged, but tells us no more and quotes no authority. However, we believe that Malcolm Canmore fought a battle at Lumphanan in 1057 when he defeated Macbeth, and he also had a residence on a small island in Loch Kinord near Dinnet. Both locations are within ten miles of Kinminity, so it is possible that the two Malcolms could have crossed paths. Let us suppose that the events that Dinnie narrates really did take place, and Malcolm goes home clutching his title deed written on a piece of Birch bark. What does he go home to? We don't know the farming arrangements at that time but he would have acquired a new and higher status than the other tenants, and this would have caused problems. He would have had to come to some arrangement with the other tenants, so that they all knew where they stood, and who got what out of the new arrangements.

That might have been possible, and things could have settled down, but a hundred or so years later, in 1170, King William the Lion decides to give all the land in Birse to the Diocese of Aberdeen, *"totas terras meas de Brass"*, together with the forests, and the natives, "my thaynes only excepted". We must assume the "natives" to be the tenants or serfs at the time, and their allegiance will have been transferred to the Diocese. If Malcolm was a Thane and if there were any other Thanes, their allegiance will have remained to the King. But there is absolutely no evidence during the whole of the period of ownership by the Diocese that there was a Lordship or Thaneship in the Parish until Bishop William Gordon conveyed a great part of Birse to his brother Alexander Gordon who built Birse Castle just after the Reformation. And even after that there is no sign of the name Malcolm in any of the records of Kinminity until 1667, when Alister and Henrietta Tayler (1933) the editors of the Spalding Edition of the Valuation Roll for 1667 narrate that *"Andrew Malcome's wife was Jean Sievewright and they had sasine 1st Dec 1668. He was portioner of Kinmunatie. James Malcome, probably his father, was in Woodend of Birse in 1625. In 1696 James Malcome son of Andrew was of Kinminity"*.

This quotation requires some comment.

1. There was a relationship by marriage between the Malcolms and the Sievewrights from at least 1668 when the Malcolms had sasine as portioners of Kinminity. Callander (2000: 9) places Jean Sievewright as a sister of "Duncan Sievewright known locally as Cutty" tenant of Midstrath, of whom we shall hear more later.

2. Andrew Malcolm's probable son, another James, portioner of Kinminity, took Sasine *"as nearest and lawful heir of deceased Andrew Malcolm in one fourth part of the Town and Lands of Kinminity"* by an Instrument of Sasine dated 11th and registered in the Register of Sasines (Aberdeen) 16th November 1685

3. In the parlance of the day the term "of Kinminity" denotes that the person is owner whereas "in Kinminity" would indicate that the person was tenant. If the term "at Kinminity" were used it would mean the person was a servant of the owner or tenant.

It is with regret therefore that we have to conclude there is no evidence at Kinminity before 1667 of a Malcolm ever being an owner or a tenant or a thane. The first evidence of the name appearing in the area is a possible Malcolm as tenant in Woodend of Birsse in 1625. Then there is Andrew Malcome's name in the 1667 Valuation Roll, and James Malcome's name as portioner of Kinminity in 1685. The "Legend of Malcolm" is thus no more than that, A Legend.

Chapter 7
The Partition of Kinminity

The tenants of Kinminity probably saw little change from the Reformation. Their leases continued, and they will have planted and reaped their crops as usual, but what Browne calls "The Partition of Birse" (Browne 1923:213) was only just beginning.

The Valuation Roll 1667. (Tayler & Tayler 1933)

The Valuation Roll for 1667 entitled "*The True and Just Valuatione off the free rent of the whole Shyre of Aberdeen commencing the first day of Jany 1667*" identifies 21 separate owners in the Parish of Birse by 1667, a figure which gradually falls back to 7 in the 18th century, but we will confine our narrative to affairs at Kinminity where we find the frequent recurrence of the names Malcolm, Turner, and Sievewright. The 21 names listed for Birse usually have the name of the property given. Quoting from the first part of the list we have six entries:-

Wm. Ross of Drumneachie	*£110-0-0*
Andrew Malcome	*33-6-8*
Jean Ross	*33-6-8*
Jeane Smith	*33-6-8*
Andrew Turner	*33-6-8*
Alex Ross of Tillysnacht	*300-6-8*

Comment here is appropriate.

1.   The first thing we notice in the whole list is that properties with under £100 rent do not show the name of the property.

2.   We know that the tenancy of Kinminity was divided into four parts in 1549, and that James Malcome took Sasine as a portioner of a one fourth portion in 1685 as nearest and lawful heir of the deceased Andrew Malcolme in $1/4^{th}$ portion of the Town and lands of Kinminity. We shall also see that the name Turner crops up later as an owner in the title deeds, and therefore we can confidently say that the four entries in the above list showing £33-6-8 are the entries for Kinminity. That there were two women Jean Ross and Jeane Smith included is unusual. Perhaps they were relicts of former occupants. Their names do not appear again, and one explanation may be that they sold their shares to the Turner family, which at one time or another appears to have owned $3/4^{th}$ portions.

3.   If we are right that the Turners owned $3/4^{th}$ portions, one of these was pledged to the Minister and Kirk Session of Birse by Bonds dated 21st January and 19th October 1646 and 22nd January 1649 (Dinnie1865:113), and eventually lost by the Turners, reducing their share to $2/4^{th}$ portions.

What happens next is the gradual acquisition of the Town and Lands of Kinminity by a variety of people.

The List Of Pollable Persons 1696.

This gives a little insight. Although there are 27 entries under Kinmonety (this was a list prepared for tax purposes, and includes servants), three entries catch our eye:-

William Turner, tenant	*17/4d*
James Malcome, his proportion	*£26-13/4d*
Poor in the Parish, portion	*£26-13/4d*

While we think we know that James Malcome was a portioner since 1685, the entry for William Turner as tenant is both puzzling and revealing. It is arguable that the Turner share should in 1696 have been twice the £26-13/4d share of the other 1/4 portions, i.e. £53-6/8d to account for William's apparent ownership of 2/4th portions, and not 17/4d as tenant. However William Turner was Clerk to the Commissioner, Francis Farquharson of Finzean, and also Tax Collector for the Parish of Birse in the 1696 Poll, so he held considerable power, particularly as to the contents of the List. If he was tenant, how did his son John complete title as owner two years later in 1698 by a Retour and Instrument of Sasine as heir to his father and ancestors? (See the section The Turner 2/4th Portions below). If William Turner performed a service to the Commissioner in compiling the List, perhaps he also performed a service to himself.

A word now about the expression "Town and Lands", and the concept of ownership of portions of the property at that time.

In a Precept of Clare Constat dated 18th Oct 1684 James Malcolm, described as Portioner of Kinminity, is served as nearest and lawful heir of the deceased Andrew Malcolm in "one fourth part of the Town and Lands of Kinminity and others" (Sasine followed in 1685). The Town was the cluster of buildings where the modern farmhouse and steading now stand, (see 1840 map Fig. 12.2) The Lands were arable ground of about 131 acres and also the moor land, rough grazing and forests which by 1840 extended to about 520 acres making an "Estate" of 651 acres. From the time of the Reformation till 1803, this sizeable piece of land was never held in single ownership, but remained divided into quarter portions of pro indiviso ownership, with the individual owners being referred to as Portioners. We shall look at the four quarter portions and see how they all eventually fell into the ownership of the Earl of Aboyne.

I.   **The Malcolm 1/4 portion.** Although Andrew Malcome's name appears in the 1667 Valuation Roll he may only have been a tenant, because Tayler and Tayler (1933) say he did not have Sasine till 1st Dec 1668. This quarter was owned by the Malcolms for a century until William Malcolm sold it to his kinsman Robert Sievewright in Cuttieshillock on 31st October 1765. This sale was still within the family and part of the deal was that Malcolm was to stay on as tenant, and in fact there were Malcolm tenants in Kinminity for another century, right through to 1856.

II. **The Turner 2/4 portions.** Two Turners had been tenants in 1511, and James Turner, described by Tayler and Tayler (1933:60) as being portioner of Kinminity in 1646, granted bonds to the Kirk Session of Birse for money lent to him during "the Troubles" (i.e. the Civil War). The Taylers describe these bords as being over "the Estate," but they were in fact only over a 1/4th portion of Kinminity. James' grandson, William, who was in Arntilliehard in 1699 raised an action to recover his estate from the Kirk after fifty years, but was unsuccessful. Meantime, in 1698, John Turner completed title to 2/4 portions by a Retour and Instrument of Sasine as heir to his father and ancestors. This, as we have seen, was just two years after William Turner's name is recorded as a tenant in the 1696 List of Pollable Persons. William must have died in 1696 or 97. After various exchanges of ownership including a John Turner, Sergeant in Lieut-General Oatways Regiment of Foot in 1742, Francis Farquharson of Finzean in 1748 and George Turner, Sheriff Clerk of Aberdeenshire, also in 1748, this George Turner conveyed the 2/4 portions to Robert Sievewright in Cuttieshillock in 1760.

III.   **The Sievewright 3/4 Portions.**   We have seen that Robert Sievewright acquired the Turner 2/4 portions in 1760 and the Malcolm 1/4 portion in 1765. These portions were conveyed to John Low who took Sasine on 29th August 1799, and John Low conveyed them to the Earl of Aboyne who took Sasine on 18th November 1803.

IV.   **The Kirk Session's 1/4 Portion.**   We have seen how the Kirk Session acquired a quarter portion from the Turner family. This is the explanation of the entry *"Poor in the Parish portion"* in the list of Pollable Persons of 1696. The Kirk utilised the rents from their portion to enable them to make payments to the poor of the parish, and in Chapter 11 we shall see how this 1/4 portion passed to the Earl of Aboyne.

Chapter 8
18th Century Farming at Kinminity

The coming of Lime.

At this point it is convenient to look at the first Statistical Account of Birse Parish (1792) by the Reverend Joseph Smith. These Statistical Accounts were produced in 1792, 1842, and 1950, and were intended to provide a picture of conditions in each Parish in Scotland in that year and their success depended on the skill and diligence of the local minister. In this case, Joseph Smith makes no reference to Kinminity, or indeed hardly any other "Township" or holding in the Parish, but rather gives a general description of conditions throughout the Parish. After estimating that there are upwards of 2000 acres under cultivation in the Parish, and dealing with soil and climate and hills and mosses, he comes to Agriculture and Produce. Here he refers to what he calls the *"prejudices against the modern improvements in husbandry".* He does allow however that some improvements have commenced in the Parish, and that some of the tenants have done more in that way than others. *"Several,"* he says, (p 7) *"have upon their possession a small limekiln; they purchase limestone at some of the quarries in the parish, and burn it with peat mixed with wood--. The lime they lay on the grounds has much effect. Some however aver, that to lime their ground is to no purpose, as, they say, it has no effect, because the ground is on limestone: Whether this be a just remark, or only an excuse for indolence, is left to the skilful farmer to decide; where a sufficient quantity of lime is allowed, it cannot fail to ensure a crop---"*

We also learn from him where they got limestone (p 20):- *"One great advantage that this Parish enjoys, is its abounding with limestone, which is to be found in many places on or near the surface. The best is at Midstrath and Ballogie* (Gallowhill). *From these quarries the tenants are chiefly supplied with the limestone which they burn at home. The greatest number of hands is employed at the Earl of Aboyne's lime-works at Birse Moor* (sic). *It is however much against the improver, that fuel is so difficult to be obtained.*

Fig. 8.1 The Lime Kiln at Midstrath

The greater part of the summer must be spent in obtaining that necessary article, consequently little of it can be spared to burn the limestone. Finding however the great benefit of lime as a manure, amazing exertions are made to procure fuel, (to burn the limestone), not only by cutting cart roads along the steep hills, to the mosses, and by purchasing wood, but even by going at times to Aberdeen for coals, which pay the high duty and must be brought across the Dee. In this case the want of a bridge at Potarch is grievously felt."

The high duty referred to was the unpopular Coal Tax which since the Act of Union in 1707 had been designed to cushion Lothian and Fife coal owners from the effects of cheap coal imports from England. This tax was abolished in the year following the Statistical Report, 1793.

There were three limestone quarries in Birse, the biggest at Mains of Midstrath, Ballogie, another at Gallowhill Wood, near Marywell, and the third at Kinminity. The whole underlying hard rock geology of that part of Birse is limestone, so the farmers who farmed in this northern part of the parish and protested that there was no need to lime their land might

Fig. 8.2 David Cochran in the disused Kinminity Lime quarry

have had a point. The huge lime kiln which survives at Midstrath, (see Fig 8.1), is now a listed building. It looks big enough to do the liming for most of the parish, but the quarry is now flooded. At Gallowhill Wood, there is also a ruinous kiln, but the quarry has become a dump for old cars and agricultural machinery. Only at Kinminity is the quarry unpolluted by water or waste, see Fig. 8.2 but the Kinminity kiln is tiny by comparison with the other two, and not enough survives to provide a meaningful illustration. It is likely that the Kinminity Kiln is one of the small ones referred to by the Minister, Joseph Smith. He does not mention the larger kilns at Midstrath or Gallowhill, so perhaps they were not in production by 1792.

It must be certain that the occupiers of Kinminity used lime on their land, because of the kiln there, identified by Simon Robson, which can be seen not 200 m to the east of the "tounship" to the south of the existing roadway. It is a semi circular stone structure fully visible on its eastern side, but very fragmentary on the west. The external diameter measures 4m, and the internal one 2.75m. Then 3.30m to the west of the kiln are the foundations of a rectangular structure measuring 4.40m x 10.30m, with evidence of an 80cm. wide doorway on the short side nearest to the kiln. This could have been a storage shed.

Cylindrical in shape, the kiln would have stood about 1.50m. high to enable top loading. Many kilns were built into a bank to facilitate loading, but surprisingly not at Kinminity, even though there is a convenient bank not far away. At the base there would have been an opening where the fire could be laid and to act as a vent, and also through which the lime could be removed.

The manufacture of lime and its use.

Lime was used by the Romans as a mortar for building, but by medieval times its use as a fertiliser had been discovered, though perhaps not fully understood. It improved the soil structure and neutralised excessive acidity, leading to increased crop yields. However, it was not until the 18th century, The Age of Improvement, that its use on the land became widespread. This is the phenomenon described by the Rev. Joseph Smith above. To make lime it was first necessary to quarry the limestone. Before 1821 this was probably done at Gallowhill, the nearest quarry. We learn from the notebook (1840-1862:4) kept by Francis James Cochran (FJC) who bought the property in 1840 that the Lime Quarry at Kinminity, shown on David Walker's Map of 1840 reproduced in Fig 12.2, was begun about 1821 or 1822. "It has hitherto been managed by James Smith" he writes in 1840, "who gets payment for his labour from those requiring lime".

We learn from page 15 of the Rental Section of the same notebook that this quarry was re-let to James Smith, the Quarrier under a seven year lease from Sept 1840 to Sept 1847 at a rent of £1-10/- pa. We also know from David Walker's map of Balfour that this James Smith was tenant of a house and six acre holding on Balfour Estate sited nearest to the Limestone quarry.

Then the limestone taken either from the Kinminity quarry, or from elsewhere will have been transported to Kinminity to the lime kiln there. The limestone will have been broken down to about half brick sized bits, and the farmers will have loaded it in to the top of the kiln along with layers of peat or wood firing. When the kiln was full, a fire was lit below and if the wind was good, all the fuel would catch, and when the temperature reached about 1000 degrees C the chemical activity took place which separated the Carbon dioxide gas from the calcium carbonate and left the lump lime or quick lime (Calcium oxide) in the kiln. From time to time over the three or four days of the burn this quick lime was emptied out, but it was an unpleasant job, as the dust was pungent to the eyes and nose. To produce a powder fit to use on the fields, the quick lime then had to be slaked by having water poured over it, which produces an extreme reaction with the danger of fire and steam and the possibility of blinding yourself. If our farmers at Kinminity survived all these dangers, they would be able to lime their land and increase its fertility and this is apparently what happened, and they continued to do so at least till the mid nineteenth century.

In 1842, The Reverend George Smith, the son of Joseph, writing in the Statistical Account of that year says *"Lime burned in the kilns at home, costs about 7d per bushel (8 gallons); that brought from Aberdeen 1s 2d, including the expense of carriage. Coals cost about 2s per barrel, the distance from Aberdeen doubling their expense"*. It is clear from this that lime burning still continued in Birse in 1842 and that even with Thomas Telford's new bridge at Potarch, the cost of importing coal from Aberdeen was still high.

Chapter 9
18th Century Happenings and Morality.

The Jacobite Rising.

Apart from the Union of the Scottish and English Parliaments, perhaps the most important public event in Scotland in the 18th century was the Jacobite Rising in 1745. The defeat of Prince Charles at Culloden led to the military occupation of large parts of Scotland including Birse by the Hanoverian Army. Not much information is available as to how all this affected Kinminity, but we can make an educated guess that one of the Turner family whom we have already met was involved.

In 1742, John Turner was served as heir to his uncle, another John Turner, in 2/4th portions of the Town and Lands of Kinminity and Sasine followed seven years later on 5th May 1749. In these documents, John Turner is described as "Sergeant in Lieut. General Oatway's Regiment of Foot". More than half of the Hanoverian army was made up of Scotsmen and it's probable that General Oatway's Regiment and Sergeant John Turner were involved at some point in action against the Jacobites.

On the other side of the divide, Callander (2000:131) quotes Birse's own Jacobite song:-

> Come, boat me owre, come row me
> owre,
> Come boat me owre to Charlie;
> I'll gie John Ross anither bawbee
> To row me owre to Charlie.

John Ross was the ferryman at Waterside, used by Kinminity at that time to get to Aboyne, and Callander names six Birse men (none of them from Kinminity) who went to join Francis Farquharson of Monaltrie (Ballater) to fight for the Prince at Culloden. History does not relate what happened to them, but Francis Farquharson, was captured and taken to London where he was condemned to death, but was pardoned and returned to Deeside thirty years later in 1776.

Within sight of Kinminity stands the house of Balnacraig, built in 1735 by its Jacobite and Catholic owner James Innes. Innes too fought for the Prince at Culloden in 1746 and escaped and returned to Deeside, but found that the house was constantly under surveillance so he lurked in a hideout nearby. In August 1746, a party of Hanoverian troops under Captain MacHardy, the officer already responsible for burning several Deeside mansions, arrived at Balnacraig. He addressed the lady of the house, Mrs Catherine Innes, saying he had come for her husband, reported to be disaffected against His Majesty King George II and demanded to see him. On being told he was not at home, he searched the house and read the Order for burning it. Catherine replied that her son Lewis was the owner and if the house was burnt the Government would be

Fig. 9.1 Balnacraig taken from Kinminity

Illus. 4. The triumph of Calvinism in the 18th Century.

held responsible as no indictment stood against the owner. This caused a problem for Captain MacHardy and Catherine suggested they have some refreshment. The Captain and his men were royally feasted and before long the cellars were emptied of their whisky and wine. The house survived and when the Redcoats eventually marched off, an eyewitness described them as "dreedfa' fu".

Well, so Wyness (1968:169) tells us. Other writers give different details, but all agree on the happy outcome. The house was not burnt and survives to this day and has been re-conditioned by the present proprietors.

It can be seen across the fields from Kinminity as is shown in Fig 9.1 It is just across the green field in the distance and the Hill of Fare is on the horizon to the right. Innes himself eventually received a pardon and died at Balnacraig in 1780.

The Kirk Session Minutes.

We have looked at the Statistical Account of Birse for 1792 and been able to glean some information about the land and the problems of farming. We shall also see from the Kirk Session Minutes how the Kirk Quarter of Kinminity came to be sold to Lord Aboyne (Chapter 11). There was another side of life in Birse which is brought sharply into focus by the Kirk Session Minutes and that is the morals of the people.

By the beginning of the 18th century, Calvinism had taken hold of most of Scotland and this included Birse. It was the job of the Kirk Session to root out all merrymaking, Sabbath breaking and immorality. Dinnie (1865) quotes three excerpts from the minutes of the beginning of the century which illustrate this:-

1701   ---- August 3rd. This day upon a complent by the minister of the frequent abuses that have happened in this parish this summer by excessive drinking and dancing at pennie bridals and that these abuses have been much fomented by   means of pypers imployed on these occasions and that John Davie in Newmill hath been frequently desired and admonished in private to forbear his pyping and being instrumental in promoting the said abuses, yet he refused to hearken unto the sd private admonitions. The session therefore appoints him to be cited before the next meeting,

1704   ---- Violet Rosse in Aldyleper, was delated for profaning the Lordsday by laying out her web to dry; Alexander Birse in Glencatt, for the crime of driving cattle from Glenesk. They are appointed to be cited to next dyet.

Marie Gardine, daughter to Francis Gardine of Midstrath delated to be with child to Gregor M'Gregor, is appointed to be cited to next dyet. The minister reports that he has a letter from the minister of Glenmuick, bearing yt he will not be persuaded to come to Birse except he be secured from Marie Gardine's friends whom he dreids for bodily harme.

Anything that gave pleasure and doing anything at all on Sunday that wasn't prayerful, had become a target for the Kirk Session to clamp down on. But the people loved roistering and drinking (Graham 1899:186/7) and most of all they loved doing it at weddings. At the "Penny Wedding" each neighbour originally contributed one penny Scots, or supplied meal, fowls or ale to plenish the feast of every young couple. Dinnie (1865:21) tells us that Penny Weddings were very common in Birse and lasted generally about five or six days, or until the goods prepared were consumed and even in some cases a fresh supply was required. The last one held in the parish was in 1840. The Church set its face against these occasions of drunkenness, profanity and sensuality and especially the promiscuous dancing of men with women. But the people called it

Fig. 9.2 The Penny Wedding
From the drawing by David Allan, Edinburgh, whose illustrations of Scots songs delighted Burns, and who did the engravings for Allan Ramsay's "The Gentle Shepherd" (1788)

"promisky" dancing and carried on regardless as the entry against the piper John Davie from Newmill shows. Violet Rosse's offence of hanging a piece of cloth out to dry at Oldyleiper on the Sabbath seems minor, but the prohibition is still deeply embedded in the Scottish Presbyterian psyche. Marie Gardine's getting with child by Gregor M'Gregor would certainly have consequences.

Attitudes softened during the century. Not all records are available, but after 1765 there are no records in Birse of people having to make public penance for Sabbath breaking or dancing, but between 9th March 1783 and 11th October 1789 twenty five young men and women from the parish, all unmarried, are brought before the Session for unclean antenuptual fornication, some more than once, (National Archives of Scotland ref CH2/595/3). Names are given, but not always addresses, so we cannot say for certain that none of them was from Kinminity. In some cases the men admitted responsibility and in some of these the parties got married. Mostly however the mother was left holding the baby though the men usually confessed in the end. When given the choice between paying a fine into the poor fund, or submitting to the Church's sanction of public discipline when they had to sit upon a stool of repentance and make penance before the whole congregation, they all chose to pay a fine, but not before being rebuked by the minister and exhorted to repentance and amendment of their life. To appear and be rebuked before the congregation was a humiliating experience which everyone tried to avoid and which could sometimes be a source of much interest and pleasure for the congregation to watch the appearance and behaviour of their neighbours in disgrace. More details of cases are given by Callander (2000:16-17). One earlier case was different and caused the Session great difficulty and the mother and the grandmother great stress. In this case, the address is given --- Drumneachie, the same *Druim an atha*, the ridge of the ford, as named by the Gaels, the same Drummenathy which King William gave to the Bishop in 1170 and the same Drumneoquhy that appeared in the Rental of 1511. It is only two farms away from Kinminity, so a very close neighbour.

On 1st March 1772	*"Ann Findlay confessed herself guilty of the sin of fornication with Alex Craig late of the Parish of Kincardine o'Neil now deceased".*
On 7th May 1772	she appeared again and *"stood by her confession. The Minister rebuked her severely for concealing and denying the matter so long, especially for not calling for proper assistance of women to help her in times of the birth so that the child died for want of care and that by law she would be considered as the murderer. The Session not knowing well how to behave in this heinous affair have however, till providence shall bring the matter to more light, appointed her to make her public appearance before the congregation to be rebuked for her aggravated sins and guilt and her mother to appear before the Session next Lord's day, neither of them for the future to have any part of the Poor money in order to deter others from the like heinous crimes".*

On 10ᵗʰ May 1772   *"Jean Aitken, mother to the above Ann Findlay*
in Drumneachie having compeared before them
and being interrogated if she knew of her daughter
being with child, if she had confest to her that she
was with child, specially if she had not felt her baby
nor knew the cause of her ailments when she was so
very ill before her delivery, lastly if she had not used
imprecations against some of her neighbours who
told her that her daughter was with child, absolutely
denied all. Whereupon the Session informed her as
they had done her daughter before that by the law
of the land her daughter were murderer of the child
for not calling for assistance in time of the birth
and therefore admonished her severely to repent and
amend her life".

The problem which faced the Kirk Session was this. As they well knew, the law of the land counted Ann Findlay's actions as murder and they explained this to Ann and her mother. Prior to 1690 juries had been reluctant to convict women of murder who concealed their pregnancy in cases where the baby died or went missing and accordingly in that year a law was passed in the following terms:- *"If any woman shall conceal her being with child during the whole space and shall not call or make use of help and assistance in the birth, the child being found dead or missing, the woman shall be holden and repute the murderer of her own child, though there be no appearance of bruise or wound upon the body of the child".*

Many women were hanged under this statute, (four in Aberdeen in 1705) and although the number had dropped off by 1772, the law was still on the Statute Book. The Kirk Session seem to have made a decision not to report the matter to the civil authorities, but to deal with it themselves.

A case from the other side of the parish is worth mentioning. In December 1773 the case of Elizabeth Anderson and Robert Harper in Balnaboth came before the Session. She confessed to the sin of uncleanness of fornication with Robert Harper. He however *"positively denied the same declaring that he never had any carnal dealings with her: whereas she affirms to his face that on the Sunday after Play Saturday at Charlestown, the rest of the family having gone to a Christening at Drumhead he dragged her into a barn and barred the door that she might not escape from his attempt upon her; the Session allowed him time to consider and he afterwards took with the Child and paid £4 Scots of penalty. They were both ordered to make their public appearance to be rebuked before the congregation. They were both afterwards absolved before the Session having paid the penalties".*

Robert Harper was born in 1757, which means he was 16 at the time of his offence with Elizabeth Anderson.

We are to meet all three parties to this story again. That is to say Elizabeth, Robert and the child.

Elizabeth came before the Kirk Session again in May 1783 for the same offence with another man, when she had to appear publicly before the congregation for two Sabbaths.

Robert was made executor by his father Francis Harper under his will dated 17th September 1790.

The child appears as a beneficiary in Francis' will in the following terms:-
"I leave and bequeath to Robert Harper junr already mentioned, a natural son of my son Robert Harper in Balnahard above mentioned the sum of Thirty Pounds sterling money, the bedding already excepted and mentioned, also the Girdle, also all my wearing apparel at my decease, also my best plaid and my clothes chest".

The Harpers had been tenants of Balnaboth since at least 1511 (280 years) and were to remain there till at least 1865 making a total of (say) 355 years. This story is a touching comment to enhance this remarkably long period of tenure. Not only did Robert sen. give his full name to his natural child, but the child's grandfather Francis, made generous and loving provision for him in his will, even to the extent of leaving him his best plaid.

Throughout Scotland the local Presbytery (in Kincardine o'Neil in this case) had oversight of the minister and would hold an annual visitation when the Session members would be interrogated about the minister. *"Is he constant in his calling or is Saturday his only book day? Does he restrain*

penny bridals? Does he preach sound doctrine?" would be some of the
questions asked (Graham 1899:333). In this way, the minister would be
in awe of his own Kirk Session. The elders had great power over the people
too, to enter their homes and enquire after their behaviour. But we can
detect a healthy resistance among the people of Birse to this interference
in their lives. Three of the young men, John Thaw, George Hunter and
Charles Ritchie, involved in paternity cases between 1783 and 1789 at
first refused to appear before the Session and John Davie refused point
blank to stop piping at Penny Bridals. It was the Kirk Session rather than
the Minister that was held in contempt by the people and it was Robert
Burns who expressed this in his biting satire "Holy Willie's Prayer"
against William Fisher, apparently a known thief and hard drinker and
an Elder of Mauchline Parish Church. Whether he was a fornicator as
well may be just Burns' poetic licence, but the poem is directed at all
hypocrites, not just Elders of the Church. Three verses are enough to
make the point.

On Penny Bridals:-

> *O Lord thou kens what zeal I bear*
> *When drinkers drink and swearers swear*
> *And singin' there and dancin' here,*
> *Wi' great and sma'*
> *For I am keepet by thy fear*
> *Free from them a'.*

And on hougmagandie (fornication):-

> *O Lord! Yestreen, thou kens, wi' Meg*
> *Thy pardon I sincerely beg*
> *O! may't ne'er be a living plague*
> *To my dishonour,*
> *An' I'll ne'er lift a lawless leg*
> *Again upon her.*

Besides I further maun allow
Wi' Lizzie's lass, three times I trow;
But ,Lord , that Friday I was fou,
When I came near her,
Or else, thou kens, thy servant true
Wad ne'er hae steered her.

The Church of Scotland's policy of public discipline gradually weakened during the 18th century as the Enlightenment spread. This led to two splits in the Church by Calvinist hard liners in 1740 and 1752 who initially had large followings, but that too gradually tailed off. By the beginning of the 19th century the Kirk started to discourage the policy of public discipline which had been central to its mission since the Reformation.

In 1792, the Rev. Joseph Smith, writing of the character of the people of Birse in the Statistical Account 1792 (p17) states. *"They are fond of social and convivial meetings; yet less addicted to drinking than they were some years ago. Indeed the young people squander much of their cash and their time in frequenting markets, marriages and other merry meetings; so that often they have not a great deal to begin with when they take up house, notwithstanding their extravagant wages. On these occasions they often hurt their morals and render themselves unfit for the duties of their stations".*

Writing in 1842, the Rev. George Smith (Statistical Accounts p 37) the son of Joseph gives the people of Birse a better report *"In point of morality, the people are generally decent and well behaved; the chief excesses whereof they are guilty arising from the abuse of ardent spirits......... In respect to religion, a just and proper value is put by the generality of the people on its ordinances and much exertion is made by those living in the distant corners of the parish to attend church".*

Chapter 10
The Reverend Joseph Smith

A native of Cromar, the Rev. Joseph Smith was minister of Birse from 2nd September 1789 to his death on 7th September 1831, a period of 42 years. Prior to his presentation to Birse as minister he was schoolmaster at Aboyne, having received his attestation by the Examinors of Candidates for the English School, Aberdeen on 6th October 1772. By the time he published the 1792 Statistical Account, he had only been in the Parish three years, yet he had clearly immersed himself in his subject and what we read there carries a certain authority and experience. He was clearly a serious person and we have read in Chapter 4 what he had to say about the Regality Courts.

But there was another side to Joseph Smith. Fifty one years after Joseph's death, Robert Dinnie (1882) published a booklet entitled "Anecdotes". Over half of these concern Joseph and in his introduction Dinnie says *"He was naturally a humorist and gave expression to many quaint and curious sayings illustrating the mode of Scottish life in years which have passed away to return no more.------ Those I have selected - although different oral versions are given - may be relied upon for their authenticity. I had occasion to be present where and when many of them were uttered by Mr Smith in his own quaint way"*. And then he adds *" -- although some of the following anecdotes may not seem to his credit, yet they did not detract from the high esteem in which he was held by all classes"*.

Here are some examples:-

Anecdote VIII   *On one occasion when catechising a boy, Mr Smith said "Weel Geordie, de ye curse ony when ye're herdin?". "Sometimes" said Geordie. "I weel believe't" said Mr Smith, "there's naething like tell the truth, man; indeed, I hae muckle adee to keep fae cursin' myself whan I'm herdin"*

Anecdote XII   *Before the blessing was announced one Sabbath in the Church of Birse, when Mr Smith was officiating, he stood up in the pulpit and said - "There is to be a catechising at Tillygarmont on Thursday first - a place that has mair need to be examined than ony ither place in this parish".*

Anecdote XXI   *At a wedding at Bottom, Finzean when the groom from Bottom neglected to kiss the bride, the minister said "Kiss her, Bottom, kiss her". (The man was better known by that appellation than by his Christian name).* We suspect Dinnie of a mischievous substitution of the place name Bottom for the farm on Finzean now called Boddam, but perhaps the spelling really has changed!

Anecdote XLVIII   *The following anecdote was told by Mr Smith himself. Meeting on the road when travelling from the Manse one day, a very young girl, he asked if she could say a prayer. "Ou aye" she said, "I can say a prayer". "That's richt" said Mr Smith, "say awa' and let's hear it". The reply was - "Matthew, Mark, Luke and John, bless the bed that I lie on".*

Joseph died in 1831 and Dinnie was born in 1808 making him 23 by the date of Joseph's death, so it is quite possible for him to have been present "where and when" many of the aphorisms were first uttered. We can read into most of the anecdotes quoted that he was a man of compassion and humour, though some of it is rather sharply expressed.

In the last chapter, we saw how the Calvinism of the Church of Scotland was diminishing from about the time Joseph first became minister at Birse and there is no record of any public disciplinary appearances before the congregation for fornication or any other offence during his ministry. However, fornication continued apace in Birse. Anecdote XLI confirms this.

The minister of Aboyne was unwell and on his behalf our Joseph went to Glentanner to perform the office of baptising a natural child. When he entered the room he saw a larger party than he expected and after looking round him he said *"Aye, aye: Is a' the fornicators of Glentanner here?" One of the company, who was an elder in the parish of Aboyne said "I dinna ken if they're a' here or no, but if a' the fornicators o' Birse were here, this room wadna haud them."*

Joseph was a product of The Enlightenment and it is clear that he spoke the Doric tongue of his parishioners whose waywardness he understood, just as they tolerated his foibles. In his school teacher's way, he gave his flock a "good" report in the 1792 Statistical Account, with just a hint of the "could do better":-

"They are active and industrious, supporting themselves and family comfortably and seem in general contented with their lot".

and

"Few in the parish have been bred to letters, yet none are illiterate".

but

"They are hospitable on all occasions; but though remarkably so to strangers, they are not fond of them settling among them".

He saw the "public discipline" policy as unproductive and he earned the respect of Robert Dinnie for his couthy humour. He brought up a son George at the Manse, who followed him into the Church and into Birse Parish as assistant from 1824 and as minister from 1831 to 1863. A plaque on the south wall of the Church commemorating them both concludes:-

"Father and son successfully discharging
The Ministerial duties of this Parish
For 74 years".

Chapter 11
Kinminity passes to the Earl of Aboyne

A considerable amount of information survives on how the sale to Lord Aboyne was effected, and is contained in the Session Records of Birse Kirk for the period between 24th October 1800 and 6th March 1803.(National Archives of Scotland CH2/595/4)

Lord Aboyne was busy acquiring the other portions of Kinminity, and he did not want to be left short of a proper title to the whole of Kinminity, which adjoined his own entailed lands to the north. On 9th October 1800 he wrote to the Kirk Session saying *"Having lately made a purchase of the lands of Kinmunnity, I feel it necessary from the manner in which these lands are runn rigged with the quarter belonging to the Kirk Session to make the two following proposals. First that I shall purchase that part belonging to the Kirk Session giving a fair and adequate price. And Secondly if that should not suit the views of the Kirk Session that our properties shall be divided at the appointment of the Court of Session at our joint expense"*.

The letter from which the above is an excerpt was considered by the Kirk Session at their meeting on 24th October 1800 and the minute records *"The Session having read and considered the foregoing letter ------ are unanimously of opinion that it would be much more for the interest of the poor of the parish to accede to the first proposal made by his Lordship rather than to incurr the expense which the Session would necessarily be led into by complying with the second"*. The Minute then proceeds *"Being uncertain as to their power to sell their property, they resolved to consult the Procurator for the Church on this point."* The Procurator agreed both to the wisdom and the legality of the sale, and the minute of the meeting on 20th April 1801 records *"The meeting taking under consideration the sale of the Sessions part of the lands of Kinmunnity (the propriety of selling these lands having been agreed to) provided a reasonable price could be got"*. The meeting then resolved to invite Mr Colin Innes to act as valuer, and he sent a letter dated 22nd Feb 1802 which makes interesting reading. He expresses the opinion that it is for the mutual advantage of the Kirk Session to sell and of the proprietor of the rest of Kinminity to buy, *"and that the price ought not to be under what may be considered a high one at present,"* but he advises the Kirk Session not to ask a price *"which may be considered exorbitant"*. He draws attention to the fact that the land is of greater value to the owner of the rest of Kinminity than to any other purchaser because the land will come in to the undivided possession of one person, and cautions against selling for too small a price, because *"some wise heads of these days will find out that the Kirk Session of Kinminity was thrown away without ever considering that none of these fields could have been brought to their then value if the sales under consideration had not taken place; who can twenty years after this describe or judge of the present real value of the Kirk Quarter when all the cairns and large stones are removed and built into dykes, all the baulks improved along with large pieces of the pasture ground into corn lands, the whole surface land out in a regular improved state. --- If this shall be the case twenty years hence, how much more shall it be fifty years afterwards"*. This letter does not advise a specific price to be asked. That must have been done by verbal communication. The matter was resolved at a meeting on 30th September 1802 when the Session agreed not to sell the land for less than £500, and when the Earl of Aboyne joined the meeting, that was exactly the price he offered.

Well, not quite! Part of the deal was that the price was to remain in the Earl's hands and interest paid @ 5%. But in the meantime the Minister received the bill from Mr Innes for his advice amounting to £10-17/6 which included a fee of £5-5/- for a plan of the subjects, which the Session did not have funds to meet It was left to the Minister The Reverend Joseph Smith to pay this bill and recover from the interest payments received from Lord Aboyne.

Chapter 12
Farming at Kinminity from 1803 to 2001

Old Tenants.

From 1803 to 1840 the land was farmed by the tenants of the Earl of Aboyne, but his sequestration was approaching and after Articles of Roup had been prepared, Kinminity came under the hammer at Advocates Hall, Aberdeen on 21st December 1840. Francis James Cochran (referred to as FJC for brevity's sake) offered the upset price of £3950 for Kinminity and was declared the purchaser. The same FJC was also successful in buying the neighbouring property of Balfour at the same price and the two properties were thereafter owned and run as one estate under the name of Balfour. The two other farms on the combined estates, namely Mains of Balfour and Oldyleiper seem to have been already modernised, or at least there was only one tenant in each, that is William Davidson in the Mains, paying a rent of £92-5/- and Peter Duncan in Oldyleiper paying £30-15/-. At Kinminity, the tenants' arable acreages (quoted here in acres, roods and perches) and rents in 1840 were:-

				Rent	
Robert Ross	19	2	3	£24	
John Malcolm	18	1	15	14	
Robert Bain	15	3	38	14	
James/ Charles Jolly	13	2	2	13	-10/-
George Sim	9	3	10	12	
George Watt		1	13	Rent not known, but later went to Craigs	
Isabel Malcolm			9	House and yard only.	
Old Mason Lodge			12	House and yard only.	
	77-	2-	22		

There were 4 roods to an acre, and 40 perches to a rood.

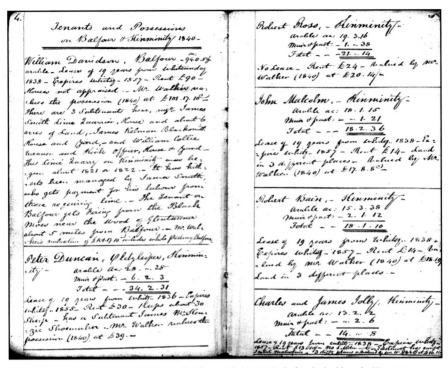

Fig. 12.1 Pages 4 and 5 of FJC's notebook compiled in 1840 before he had bought Kinminity.

The rent can be seen to vary above and below £1 per acre. Pages 4 and 5 of the notebook compiled by FJC are reproduced at Fig. 12.1 which show some of the above details taken from the sale particulars of the property. This notebook will be referred to again in relation to other matters it contains.

The only name we find in this list surviving from the previous centuries is Malcolm, whose family it will be remembered was related by marriage to the Sievewright family, who owned 3/4th portions of Kinminity from the 1760's to 1799.

It was on the occasion of the sale by the Trustees of the Earl of Aboyne to FJC that David Walker's map of the whole of the town and lands of Kinminity was prepared. A part of that map is reproduced at Fig 12.2

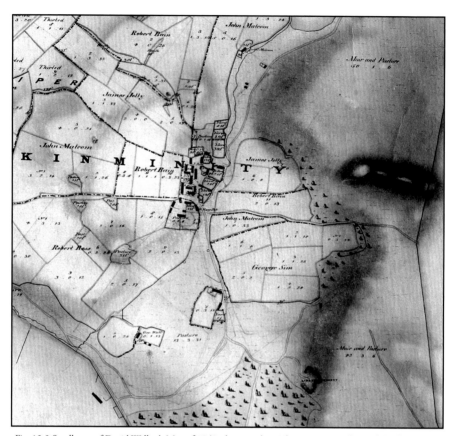

Fig. 12.2 Small part of David Walker's Map of 1840, showing the 18th century township and the field layout with tenants' names and the Lime Quarry. The cluster of 20 structures can be clearly seen. In addition, each tenant had a small area (up to 6 acres) of pasture and there were 362 acres of common pasture and 164 acres of natural wood. The dark crescent shaped feature, lower right, is the Limestone Quarry.

David Walker's plan, besides being a document of considerable historic interest, is also a thing of beauty. It measures four feet ten inches by two feet and has the arable land coloured light yellowy brown, the moorland and pasture coloured a light blue green and the woodland a darker blue green, but with no contours. Instead, crags and hillocks are shaded in black. The surveying has been very thorough and as far as can be seen today the plan is accurate.

Fig. 12.3 Francis James Cochran who was 31 years old in 1840 when he bought Kinminity and Balfour.

New Tenants.

Between 1840 and 1857 great changes took place at Kinminity. We learn something about what was going on during this period from FJC's notebook (pp 123 and 126) but not everything. The quotation and the actual price paid for the Kinminity "offices" (that is the steading building) are given, but not those for the farmhouse. This suggests that the farmhouse may have already been built by 1840 and on David Walker's map there is a structure shown where the farmhouse now stands, which could be it.

The entries in the notebook for the "offices" are as follows:-

Page 123:
1857 April 6
Offers accepted for new offices at Kinminity vizt,
William Duguid Wright, Aboyne for

	Mason work	*£121-14- 0*
	Carpenter etc	*37-10-0*
	Plaster work	*4-18-0*
	Ashphalt etc	*8-5-0*
	Threshing mill	*33-10-0*
		£205-17-0
John B Innes for		
	slater work	*63-18-0*
		£269-15-0

Page 126:
1858 Jany 7
Total cost of new offices at Kinminity
All the work except the slater work,
Wm. Duguid Wright Aboyne

		£205-17-0
	Slater work, J B Innes	*63-18-0*
	Wood	*45-10-0*
	Sawing do	*20-14-10*
Extra work	*W Duguid*	*£3-2-0*
	R Smith extra sawing	*£4-0-3*
	Wood	*4-17-0*

Here FJC's notes end. The total can be seen to be the original estimate of £269-15-0 plus the extras for wood and sawings. If we have read the date of payment right, the work was completed between April 1857 and January 1858.

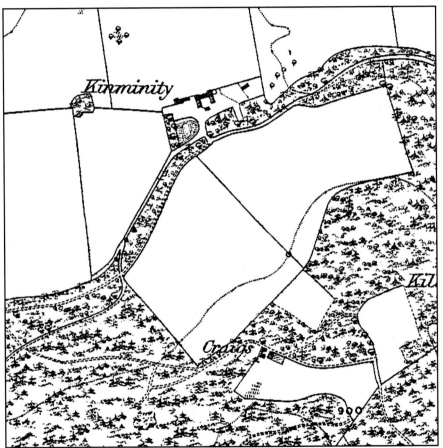

Fig. 12.4 Kinminity from the 1867 Ordnance Survey Map

All this happened just after the appearance of the Second Statistical Account in 1842. Here the Rev George Smith gives us a general view of the whole Parish without mentioning Kinminity, but he does mention that the number of arable acres in the Parish is about 3360 acres. This compares with the figure of about 2000 acres given by his father Joseph in 1792, so it appears that the improvers had made considerable progress in the previous fifty years.

All structures on the 1840 plan not within the township have disappeared by 1867, save one, and that is the cottage un-named on the 1840 map but called Craigs on the 1867 O.S. Map (see Fig 12.4 and Chapter 14 below). It can be seen to the south of Kinminity, across the fields. Other changes are that two field enclosures have been made next to the cottage at Craigs out of what was formerly muir and pasture.

All the leases outstanding in 1840 had expired by 1857 and a lease of Kinminity was granted in 1857 to Charles Jolly at an annual rent of £65 for nineteen years of the lands formerly let to George Sim, Robert Ross, Charles Jolly himself, (and his brother James Jolly), John Malcolm and Robert Bain. We are not certain whether the house was new, but the steading was and was paid for by January 1858 and also many of the field boundaries had been extended and squared off. For the first time in its history, Kinminity was in single ownership and apart from Craigs Cottage occupied by a single tenant.

1857 was the year by which all the existing leases had run out and the years from 1840 must have been an anxious time for the tenants. We don't know how old they were and some may have been due for retirement anyway by 1857. However they will all have witnessed the demolition of the Tounship and the building of the new steading and the re-arrangement of the land boundaries. What we do know is that in 1857 George Sim got a lease of Craigs and Charles Jolly got a lease of the farmhouse and steading and 59 acres out of the rest of the Kinminity land.

One observer of these events who put his thoughts into words was Robert Dinnie (1865:64). With his eye perhaps on the fact that John Malcolm's lease was not renewed and that he clearly thought that there had been Malcolms in Kinminity since the days of Malcolm Canmore, (see The Malcolm Legend Chapter 6) he makes the reproachful comment *"---there is but little respect paid to old tenants of this class by the majority of the present proprietors".*

Fig. 12.5 Kinminity Steading as disused in 2001 showing the cattle court on the left.

Fig. 12.6 Kinminity Steading East as renovated 2005.

The Reverend George Smith the author of the Second Statistical Account in 1842 expresses satisfaction over the completion of the Bridge over the Dee at Potarch, the want of which was so grievously felt by his father in 1792 (see Chapter 8) and as mentioned, he records that the arable acres in the Parish have increased to 3360.

Since its rebuilding in the 1850's Kinminity Farm continued to be occupied by a single tenant, until 2001. For at least 50 years the tenants had security of tenure under the Agricultural Holdings (Scotland) Act 1948 and to a limited extent before that. In 1950, the Rev Robert K Williamson published the Third Statistical Account. By this time the arable land in the Parish has increased to 4796 acres, with approximately half of it in grass. Williamson comments (p 47) that several farms have erected covered courts for wintering cattle. Kinminity was one of these (see Fig 12.5). The second half of the Twentieth Century was a period of relative prosperity for farmers, when amalgamations were encouraged and in this period Kinminity re-acquired some of the land at Oldyleiper which had been separated off at an earlier time.

Leases and rents up to 2001 were:-

1857 - 1875	Charles Jolly	£65
1875 - 1890	James Jolly	£72
1890 - 1916	James Coutts	£62
1916 - 1926	Robert Copland	not known
1926 - 1934	Charles Williams	£62
1934 - 1946	Andrew Reid	£30
1946 - 1965	George Beveridge	£50
1965 - 1972	G D Logie Beveridge	£305
1972 - 1979	do do	£452
1979 - 1984	do do	£1200
1984 - 2001	do do	£2300

When Logie Beveridge's tenancy terminated in 2001, the farm fell vacant
and planning permission was obtained for the conversion of the steading
into two dwelling houses. Fig. 12.5 and Fig. 12.6 show the condition of
the steading in 2001 and 2005.

Chapter 13
Communications

The South Deeside Road.

From the start, there has always been access to and from Birse and Kinminity in all directions, though it has not always been easy. The Cairn o'Mount and Fir Mounth crossings are believed to date from Neolithic times. In the historical period, distinguished visitors have always been able to get here if they wished. St Colm came here over the Firmounth in the 5th century, Macbeth and Malcolm Canmore both came here with armies in 1057. In 1170 Kinminity began a direct link with the Bishop of Aberdeen and the Bishop may have come to a Hunting Lodge near Balfour. Armies marched over the Mounth and up and down Deeside during the Wars of Independence and the Civil War and the Jacobite Risings. We are going to focus on the South Deeside Road which was the main road from Aboyne to the Cairn o' Mount crossing. Kinminity stood astride this road.

The Reverend George Smith states the position in 1842 in simple terms (Statistical Accounts p 40). There was the Great North Road from Whitestone to Potarch and there was the South Deeside Road from Whitestone to the suspension bridge at Aboyne. These are the Red and Green roads shown on our Roadmap.

Callander (2003) has done a detailed study of the roads and tracks in Birse in which he cautions that " --- *the details of some of the routes identified and the interpretation of their significance, should be treated as somewhat speculative pending further research".* With regard to the South Deeside Road (which up to the late 18th century actually went through Kinminity) he says *"It is not clear when this old route was replaced by the current line of the B976, but it appears to have occurred in a number of stages by the mid 19th century".* This is confirmed by the terms of David Walker's map of 1840. Although it is shown as a road south of Kinminity township, it is not shown at all between Kinminity and Oldylieper. It is

Fig. 13.1 The double dykes where the South Deeside Road crosses to Glencat and on to Cairn o'Mount

Fig. 13.2 The South Deeside Road, looking south, where it enters the former Kinminity township

therefore impossible for it to have been used as a road by 1840.

Fig. 13.1 shows the double dykes flanking this road as they are today near Craigs Cottage.   They are 4.5 m. apart and built in the 18th century trapezoidal style which we will examine more closely in the next chapter.

David Walker's 1840 map Fig 12.2. shows a road going down from here across the open field directly through the Kinminity township and if we go there we find another set of double dykes now used as the access to the east steading. These are 8m. apart and are shown in Fig. 13.2. We could expect to find the road wider at the point where it goes through the farm complex and that is exactly what is there. These dykes are a little more perpendicular in shape which may mean they were built later than those up on the hill.   This road was disused by 1840, but in its day it was clearly a road of major importance. The interesting fact is however that from time immemorial right up to the early 19th century, anyone travelling from Aboyne (or Bonty as it was before the 17th century) to anywhere south by the Cairn o' Mount, or in the opposite direction, would have passed right through the township of Kinminity. This applies to travellers by foot or hoof and perhaps coaches too, and also to armies and explains to some extent the siting of the "fort" at Kildordy which is on top of a hill not 200 m from the road. From there, the garrison had complete control of the road.

We have referred earlier to the curious fact that whereas   in the lawless period following the Reformation, nearly every other farm in the Parish fell into the ownership of a major or minor local baron, Kinminity remained in the possession and later ownership of the tenants. One explanation could be that nobody wanted a farm that posed such a temptation to the travelling public. Theft and violence are two obvious hazards from having a farm in such a situation.

Other Roads.

In other directions there was a variety of roads. The main roads to the West, North and East were all on the North of the Dee and this involved crossing the river. In early Christian and medieval times, this would have been by the Belwood Boat. Up to the mid 18th century, Callander (2003) reports the use of a ferry at Waterside which was about opposite where Bonty would have been. From the 18th century this was moved west to the Inn beside the current Aboyne bridge, now remembered in the name of the Boat Inn. For local travel there was a network of internal roads within the parish, one of which passing near to Kinminity was the Church or Coffin Road from the Forest of Birse, already referred to and coloured violet on the Roadmap. Callander (2003) suggests that this road was only used by church goers and coffin bearers from the early 18th century when the Forest of Birse became permanently settled. Another track used by

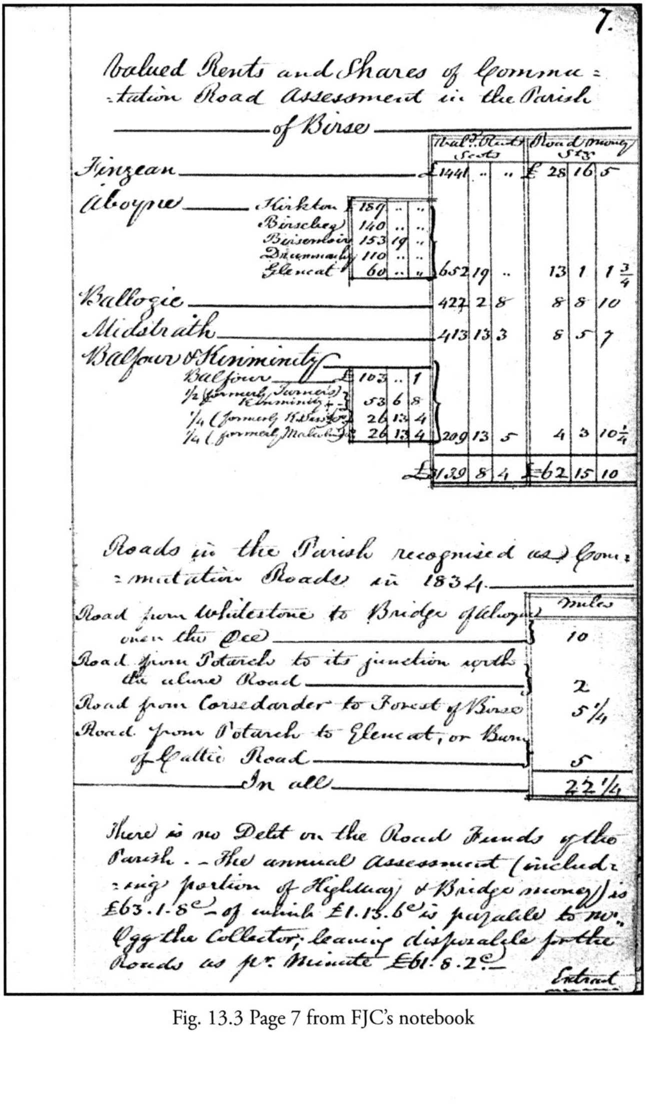
7.

Valued Rents and Shares of Commutation Road Assessment in the Parish of Birse

					Val^d. Rent Scots			Road money Stg		
Finzean					£1441	..	..	£ 28	16	5
Aboyne	Kirkton	£189	..	..						
	Birsebeg	140	..	..						
	Birsemore	153	19	..						
	Drummachy	110	..	..						
	Glencat	60	..	..	652	19	..	13	1	1 3/4
Ballogie					427	2	8	8	8	10
Midstrath					413	13	3	8	5	7
Balfour & Kinminity	Balfour	£103	..	1						
	1/2 (formerly Turner's) Kinminity	53	6	8						
	1/4 (formerly ...)	26	13	4						
	1/4 (formerly ...)	26	13	4	209	13	5	4	3	10 1/4
					£3139	8	4	£62	15	10

Roads in the Parish recognised as Commutation Roads in 1834

	Miles
Road from Whitestone to Bridge of Aboyne over the Dee	10
Road from Potarch to its junction with the above Road	2
Road from Corsedarder to Forest of Birse	5 1/4
Road from Potarch to Glencat, or Burn of Cattie Road	5
In all	22 1/4

There is no Debt on the Road Funds of the Parish. – The annual Assessment (including portion of Highway & Bridge money) is £63.1.8^d – of which £1.13.6^d is payable to M^r. Ogg the Collector, leaving disposable for the Roads as p^r. Minute £61.8.2^d. –

Extract

Fig. 13.3 Page 7 from FJC's notebook

Illus. 5. The coming of the railway to Aboyne in 1859.

Kinminity farmers to exercise their rights of grazing in the Forest of Birse was up the Burn of Birse past Newmill, coloured brown on the Roadmap.

As Callander (2003) points out, the Cairn o'Mount road through the eastern side of Birse to what became Potarch Bridge was the main road from the south. It was the Great North Road (coloured red on the Road Map) and stretched all the way from Edinburgh to Inverness. It is 6.5m wide where it can be seen where it goes through the Forest of Slewdrum. There was a major improvement there when the bridge was built at Potarch in 1814 not only for the North/South travellers, but also for those at Kinminity needing to go to Aberdeen. We have seen how the Minister in 1792 cried out for a bridge to be built there. Kinminity was within three miles of The Great North Road at Potarch and astride the branch road leading from it to Aboyne. It was therefore not isolated and on occasion must have been the first in the area to hear any dramatic news from the south. However the boom in traffic along that road was not to last for long after the bridge at Potarch was built. When the railway reached Aboyne in 1859 the easiest way south was by train to Aberdeen and then southwards. Kinminity was comparatively more isolated after 1859 than it had been throughout its previous existence.

At this point, it is worth looking more closely at p.7 of FJC's note book, shown in Fig. 13.3.

This early part of the book was written before he bought Kinminity and are his notes about what he was hoping to buy. On p.7 he was writing down what his liabilities would be for maintenance of the roads in the parish. It can be seen that in the left hand column he notes the Valued Rents in pounds Scots for all the heritors (landowners) in the parish, including Kinminity and to the right the Road Money in Sterling, presumably what each heritor would have to pay. The Valued Rent was not what you had to pay, but was rather a notional value to compare with other properties so that the amount of tax payable by you could be fixed. Those of us who remember paying rates on our houses will also remember that we all had a Rateable Value and that our Rates bill was fixed by reference to that.

So it was with the Valued Rent and those readers with good eyesight and attention to detail will notice that the Valued Rent figures for Kinminity in the notebook of 1840, are exactly the same as the valuations of the proportions of land at Kinminity in the 1696 List Of Pollable Persons quoted in Chapter 7, except that the figure for the Turner portion is given as £53-6/8, which we argued it should have been all along.

Chapter 14
The House that Cutty built

A general description.

Craigs Cottage has been briefly mentioned in this account in Chapter 12. It is shown but not named on David Walker's map of 1840 and no arable land went with it at that date. Yet the 1867 O.S. map (Fig. 12.4) names it and shows two areas of arable land next to it. FJC's notebook (p.16 of the Rental Section) shows it as let to George Watt for 19 years from Whits 1846 at a rent of £2-5/- pa for the first eleven years and £3 thereafter when the whole area had been trenched (ploughed). The 1864/65 Valuation Roll shows George Sim as occupier under a lease of less than 19 years and this suggests that George Watt may have died before the expiry of his lease. The records do not show what happened or who lived there before 1846 or after George Sim, but the assumption is that the unit became unviable in the late 19th century and was abandoned. This would not be surprising because the situation is high, the acreage small and access difficult. The house was derelict in the early 20th century and the land was planted over with trees in the 1950's.

Writing in 1865, Dinnie (1865:9-11) , describing the buildings in Birse of *"upwards of a hundred years ago"* says that the farmers' and cottagers' houses were built of natural faced stones that could be obtained nearest the site. He gives a fairly detailed description of the style of building , with most of which Craigs Cottage can be said to conform, but of most interest is the description of the fire places. He says *"The fireplaces had no chimneys built into the walls to direct the smoke; but what was called a backstone of five feet in height was built to the gable wall and the fire placed before it. The smoke went up the side of the wall and out at a large wooden "lum" or chimney top, with an opening of two feet square."* Callander (2000:27-28) gives a brief history of hangin' lums in Birse. For years the people of Birse cooked over an open fire set on the floor in the centre of their living space, the smoke finding its way out through a hole in the

Fig. 14.1 The internal south gable of Craigs Cottage showing traces of smoke blackening.

thatched roof. The first "modernisation" was to set up a large stone on one side of the fire and place a wooden box in the roof hole The next was to move these and the fire to the gable wall. Callander then describes the development of the hanging lum, which was a funnel arrangement like an inverted hopper that hung over the fire and carried the smoke directly up. It was constructed of wood and clay and the bottom end of the canopy was supported on wooden joists projecting from the gable wall. Callander then says that it was recorded in 1791 that there were no slated farmhouses in the parish and that the houses had the upper half of each gable built of turf. Many of these houses were modernised during the nineteenth century and it was at this time that the "hanging lum" started to disappear.

The photograph at Fig. 14.1 shows the south gable of Craigs Cottage as it survives today. A blackened area can be seen near the ground and traces of blackening above that, but there is no sign of a backstone. Fenton (1981:21-27) describes the transition from the central hearth with a

Fig. 14.2 Cross section of a dyke with gable of Craigs cottage in the background.

backstone to the chimney in the gable. At different times during the 18th Century in different parts of Scotland, the grate was moved to the gable and sometimes the backstone was retained to protect a turf wall, but often it was dispensed with when the gable, as at Craigs, was built in stone. Chimneys in the gable became standard in the 19th century, which means that Craigs was probably built in the last quarter of the 18th Century.

But why were proper internal gable chimneys not built? Such chimneys had been built in Scotland for hundreds of years and there is many a medieval castle ruin around to prove it. Cost must be the main reason, but Fenton (2001:5) suggests another. *"Sensitivity about smoky conditions"* he tells us *"is a relatively modern phenomenon. It is clearly shown by the long survival of the central hearth in the kitchens of blackhouses and other types of home in the north and west of Scotland that the occupants of such houses were not particularly worried by smoke"*. That of course was before the arrival of coal as a household fuel, but coal will have been a late arrival in Birse except for industrial use in the lime kilns.

Next to the cottage is a drystone dyke (Fig. 14.2) stretching eastwards to join the South Deeside Road, (see Chap 13). The dyke is quite unlike a nineteenth century dyke. It is trapezoidal in shape being at least twice as wide at the bottom as at the top. We can learn something of when and how this dyke may have been built from a contract between the Earl of Aboyne and James Masson in Tillyjouck dated 11ᵗʰ March 1756 to build a similar dyke in part of the Forest of Birse belonging to the Earl. (Aboyne Muniments Ref GD181). The dyke in that contract was to be five 'quarters' high, three foot wide at the base, eighteen inches wide at the top and covered with a cope of turf. If a "quarter" was a quarter of a yard, then five quarters would be 45 inches.   In cross section, that was trapezoidal, which is just what we find at Craigs. The measurements at Craigs are about the same as mentioned in the Masson contract, but in places they are up to six feet wide at the base, five feet high and three feet six inches wide at the top.

The other terms of the contract, though a diversion, make interesting reading. All 18ᵗʰ century grammar and mis-spellings are faithfully reproduced:-

Mr Masson is *"to engage three sufficient hands to build with himself and also six lads for holling and carting stones and to uphold the builders in hamers and tools he is to enter to the work with the foresaid builders and servants precisely the twenty six day of May next and to continue thereafter thirteen weeks or a full quarter of a year. For which the said Hary Gordon* (the Earl's factor) *in name and account of the said Earle of Aboyn Here by become bound and obliged to pay to the said James Masson one penny farthing Sterland for each Scots Ell of the above Dyke so to be builded with a peck of meall to every thirty els and Fourty three pounds Scots of the wages of the above six lads with two pecks of oat meall at eight stone weight the boll with half a peck of malt weekly to each of the said six lads as there entertainment and to afford them tooles for holling the stones carte horses and borrow for leading them and this in name of everything the said James Masson can ask or demand of the said Hary Gordon or the said Earle of Aboyn for performing the above written engagement and if it shall happen that through there being plenty of money found about some part of the said dyke mor than others the said James Masson obliges himself that the hollers and carters shall not by*

finding such plenty slacken there diligence in drawing and carting but go on at the same rate as if they were keeping the dyker onley at constant worke".
It's not all easy to understand but we think we recognise that Mr Masson was not to let the haulers and carters slacken their diligence if they found they had more stones than they needed.

Why and by Whom was it built?

If we are right that the house was built in the last quarter of the 18th century, more interesting questions are why was it built and by whom? There has obviously been some connection with Kinminity for it lies just one field away from the township, with access up to it before 1840 by the South Deeside Road. We have seen that George Watt got a 19 year lease of Craigs in 1847, along with the newly trenched acres of land round it. There is no entry in the sale particulars or anywhere else in 1840 showing anyone paying rent for Craigs.

Our acquaintanceship with the titles of Kinminity, leads us to the conclusion that Craigs was built sometime between 1765 and 1799 by the "laird" of Kinminity, Robert Sievewright who as we have seen (Chap 7) acquired the Turner 2/4 portions of Kinminity in 1760 and the Malcolm 1/4 portion in 1765. He may only have been laird of 3/4 portions, the other quarter still belonging to the Kirk, but that need not have stopped him building a house there. What an opportunity for him to build a residence for himself, on a site where he could look down on his landed estate! And a closer look at the ruin suggests that this is not a house built for a tenant farmer, but has an element of quality about it. Look at the mortar work on the stonework of the gable and the coping stones, (Fig 14.1). It is well built and has survived over 220 years of exposure to the elements, whereas a house built for a tenant farmer or farm worker would probably only have a turf gable. There is a window on the right of the gable and the writer remembers that above that window there was another very small window (now collapsed) which suggests an upper landing. The only person with an interest and a title to build it in the later years of the 18th century was Robert Sievewright.

So who was this Robert Sievewright whose family has been related by marriage to the Malcolms of Kinminity since 1668 ?

The first Sievewright known to us, Duncan, was tenant of Midstrath in Glencatt and had a sister married to the Malcolm "laird" of Kinminity in the 1660's. Callander (2000:9) assigns the name Cutty to him, but the matter is complicated by Tayler and Tayler (1933:59), when in their Introduction they state "there were Malcolms in Kinminity, Birse down to 1760 when it also was sold to one Sievewright, son of Cutty".

There are therefore three possible Cutties:-

Cutty I.	Duncan, tenant of Midstrath in the 1660's named as Cutty by Callander.
Cutty II	The father of "one Sievewright", referred to by Tayler and Tayler. We think this was Robert "the elder" referred to in the titles.
Cutty III	Robert, younger son of Robert "the elder", named Cutty, as we shall see below, by Dinnie (1882). It was this Cutty who bought 3/4th portions of Kinminity in the 1760's.

Sources indicate that Duncan (Cutty I) was an enterprising and entrepreneurial individual who married well and borrowed 2000 merks to buy Drumneachie in 1696. He had two sons, James and Francis, neither of whom came forward as heirs to his estate because of the debts, and Francis later signed back Drumneachie to clear the debt. Then, we have Robert "the elder", (Cutty II), referred to by Tayler and Tayler. And finally, we have the Cutty we are really interested in, Robert, his son (Cutty III). When he bought 2/4th portions of the Town and Lands of Kinminity from George Turner in 1760, he is described in the title deed as "younger son of Robert Sievewright elder in Cuttieshillock".

Five years later in 1765, this Robert Sievewright (Cutty III) described as "Robert Sievewright in Cuttieshillock" buys 1/4th portion of Kinminity from William Malcolm. So we are nearly able to trace the family tree of the Sievewrights:-

> In the 1660's Duncan Sievewright's (Cutty I) sister Jean marries Andrew Malcolm either then or soon to be "of" Kinminity.
>
> In 1696 Duncan buys Drumeachie with borrowed money which has to be signed back on his death.
>
> One of his two sons James or Francis becomes father of Robert Sievewright the "elder" (Cutty II).
>
> Robert the "elder's" younger son Robert (Cutty III) buys 2/4th portions of Kinminity from George Turner in 1760, and another 1/4th portion in 1765 from his kinsman William Malcolm.

The likely explanation of there being so many Cutties is that whichever Sievewright was the tenant of Cuttieshillock betweeen the 1660's and the 1760's was known as Cutty. This leaves open the possibility that there was another Cutty, ie either James or Francis, whichever was the father of Cutty II, but so far we have no written reference to him under that name.

Dinnie's (1882) Anecdotes have already been introduced to the reader. These are mostly about the minister Joseph Smith, but Anecdote LXXV is about Cutty Sievewright, (Cutty III). It reads as follows and remember that Dinnie was writing in the 1880's:-

"An old saying which was often repeated in the Parish of Birse and also the neighbouring localities about one hundred years ago, is now but seldom used among the present generation. When anything was given away and was expected to return, or be returned the saying was:- "Its like Cuttie's note, it'll come again", which had its origin from a person whose surname was Sievewright, although better known by the appellation of "Cuttie" having resided many years at Cuttieshillock in the neighbourhood of Birse -- his native parish. He was also proprietor of a part of Kinminity in the Parish of Birse which he purchased from the Malcolms in the year 1760; but sold it in

a few years after. On one occasion a creditor applied to "Cuttie" for a one
pound note appearing to be much in want of it at the time. "Cuttie" in place
of a bank note, presented an old "permit" which the person accepted without
making any remark -- "Cuttie" saying at the same time -- "It'll come again, it'll
come again" from which arose the phrase "It'll come again like Cuttie's note".
I may observe that several people at that time were not so much accustomed
to seeing pound notes as they are at the present and could not distinguish them
from a document ornamented in some sort of similar form".

Some parts of this anecdote can now be instantly verified:-

> Robert Sievewright (Cutty III) was "in" Cuttieshillock
> at that time as the title deeds of 1760 and 1765 confirm.
> Cuttieshillock is outwith the parish of Birse, but is
> in its "neighbourhood" and his family's residence at
> Midstrath makes Birse his "native parish".
> He was also proprietor of a part of Kinminity from
> 1760 and he sold it " few years after" in 1799.

Cuttieshillock was then an Inn standing on the Great North Road (see
Roadmap) a mile south of the Feugh Bridge or crossing at Whitestone,
so there was a direct road between Cuttieshillock, Midstrath, Craigs and
Kinminity along the South Deeside Road. The road goes within 200 m.
of Craigs Cottage, before reaching Kinminity. We now know Robert
Sievewright the Younger, "in" Cuttieshillock to be Dinnie's Cutty, or
Cutty III. We are also convinced that it was he who built Craigs cottage
between 1760 and 1799. All we lack is a direct written reference linking
Cutty to Craigs.

Cutty had the same financial instincts as his great grandfather, Duncan,
in the previous century. Like Duncan, he had to sell the property after a
few years. And other things went wrong for him. When Francis Harper

in Balnaboth died in December 1790, his executors were authorised to collect a Bill for £21 dated 16th May 1789 due by Robert Sievewright in Cuttieshillock (Cutty III) for which there was a decree registered in the Kincardine Sheriff Court Books on 21st Dec 1789 and it wasn't so easy for Cutty to pass a piece of printed paper to the Sheriff Clerk and tell him "It'll come again, it'll come again". Dinnie's anecdote shows him to be something of a rogue, though from the way it is told a likeable rogue. You can read affection into the joke that "It'll come again like Cutty's note". It just seems to mean that when you were with Cutty, you had to keep your wits about you.

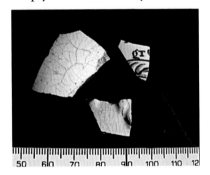 

Fig. 14.3 Photos of Artefacts.

Four artefacts and a piece of coal were found on the floor of the house in 1997 all within a foot of each other following a very brief scrape under the turf. There was a piece of deer horn and three shards of table ware. Two of the latter are good quality glazed and decorated china. They could of course have belonged to George Watt or George Sim, the subsequent tenants, but we don't really want to believe that. Far better that we can look at Craigs and the finds and think of Cutty, this larger-than-life, sleight-of-hand character with the memorable name and the up-market tea set, living (with a wife?) in our now quiet and deserted and melancholy ruin.

Chapter 15
Looking back from the 21st Century

Long Occupation by Families.

Fig. 15.1
Logie Beveridge, the last tenant of Kinminity Farm

The retirement from farming by Logie Beveridge in 2001 brought to an end 55 years of occupation of Kinminity by his family since his father first became tenant in 1946. Logie is shown in Fig. 15.1 standing outside the house he occupied for so long and the house itself appears in Fig. 15.2 This is a spell which may not match that of the Turners (1511 to 1760, 249 Years) or the Malcolms (1667 to 1857, 190 years), but it reflects the continuing tradition of long term association with their land by farmers in Birse in general and Kinminity in particular. One family in Birse which exceeds the Turners is the family we have already met, the Harpers who were in Balnaboth, Finzean from 1511 to at least 1865 (say 355 years).

History in Kinminity.

Proven occupation of the land at Kinminity for hundreds of years by one family is one thing but 4000 years of human occupation in that area is something else. We can but reflect on the possibility that some of the direct descendants of those prehistoric peoples are among the families we have come across.

In pre-history we know nothing about the inhabitants except their

Fig. 15.2 Kinminity Farmhouse as it stands today

artefacts, a knife and an arrowhead. The Pictish people have left us nothing but a fragment of a carved stone. When St Colm arrived carrying the Gospel of Christianity how did they react? We don't even know what language they spoke, except that it was probably a Celtic language related to Welsh. They never wrote it down. How can we know what sort of a welcome they gave to St Colm? In what language did he communicate with them? Did he effect mass conversions of a whole tribe, or did he baptise individuals one by one? And then in the ninth century, a new culture arrived, Gaelic. Did the Picts move out and the Gaels move in? Probably not. More likely Gaeldom took over without slaughtering or expelling the Picts. The Gaelic culture was literate, more vibrant and brought contact with the rest of the British Isles and Europe and with Rome and its Church, in place of the Celtic Church brought by St Colm and St Columba. Although the scribes who wrote the Book of Deer in the 9th century wrote in Latin, they wrote marginal comments in Gaelic. The dwellers in Kinminity will have just accepted the new culture. They wouldn't have much choice. They learned to speak the new language and to call their farm *caenn monaidh*, until in another 250 years a lawyer

Illus. 6. Mid 20th Century farming.

wants to know how to spell it so the farm can be given by the King to the Bishop. It seems no-one could spell it any more, because everyone was speaking a new language from England. There were no literate Gaels

Fig. 15.3 Kinminity Steading as it is today

left to tell him so he just put down Kinmonty and it has hovered at something near that ever since.

And did being tenants of the Bishop make a difference to their lives? Probably not. They seem to have suffered from the same intrusions as everybody else and perhaps more so because of their position on the main road. Armies and caterans will have paid no attention to the fact that this was Church land. They will have looted and stolen just the same.

Then came the Reformation. It is difficult for us from the present time to appreciate what a cataclysmic event this was. John Knox struck at the Roman Catholic Church in Scotland with a ferocity barely equalled in Europe. On one day in 1560, Calvinism became the order of the day and it became a crime punishable by death to be caught saying or hearing Mass for the third time. Churches were desecrated, Church treasures were stolen and Church land was grabbed by the strong. And that was only the start. For the next two hundred years, wars of religion were fought and the Civil War and the Jacobite rising can be counted among them. North east Scotland was spared the worst of these and one can even ask if the Kinminity tenants noticed the Reformation. Certainly, as they lived within half a mile or so from the Church, they can hardly have missed the change from priest to minister, or more likely, no minister for a long time. And if they went to Church they will have noticed the different form of service.

But whether it made any difference to their life on the farm is doubtful. However, 85 years later in 1645 a body of soldiery loyal to the Duke of Montrose arrived at Kildordy. Now, one of the attractions of being a soldier in those days was the opportunity it gave for a bit of rape and pillage. There were almost certainly four families living in Kinminity then, along with their servants and they were the very nearest place to Kildordy, not more than half a mile down the South Deeside Road. It's all surmise of course, but it would be surprising if at the very least the soldiers did not make off with a fair quantity of food, not to mention any other liberties they may have taken.

By this time the four farmers were beginning to become owners of shares in the land, but the Civil War was upon them and if they had to join in, on which side? Some fathers are known in Scotland to have sent one son to support each side so at least one of them would be on the winning side. And all the time up to 1748 the Regality Court was exercising its dreaded jurisdiction in the Parish.

By the 18th century, written titles abound and farming was being improved. We have seen how in 1792, the talking point in the Parish was whether to lime your land or not. It seems that in the end, most did and Kinminity was up there with the leaders in having its own lime kiln. The arrival of Cutty Sievewright in the 1760's must have been another talking point. The new owner and his reputation would be known to all the tenants and his decision to build a house up in the woods will have been followed with keen interest. He probably employed many of them to help build it. And if he paid them in counterfeit money, they will have consoled themselves -- "It'll come again, it'll come again".   If we want to know the other talking points, the best source we have is the Kirk Session minutes. Who was fathering whose child? Who would be publicly rebuked in church next Sabbath? Who to get as piper for your daughter's Penny Bridal?

Kinminity Today.

The 19th and 20th centuries are periods of steady progress, mostly for the good. A proper farm house and steading were built and although some of the tenants had to leave, those that were able to stay had a better life. Francis James Cochran planted hundreds of trees including 350 Beech, 350 Elm, 300 Plane and 350 Ash, (listed in his notebook p 54) and some of these can still be seen round Kinminity and on the avenue running past it.

The land at Kinminity is still farmed but by neighbouring farmers and the steading has been converted to two dwelling houses by two great great great grandsons of Francis James Cochran, David Cochran and Mark Robson.

Nothing has been found of the township which was once there save some shards of tableware now kept at Kinminity. The site is one of great beauty, facing south and with open views to the north towards Lumphanan and the hills of mid Deeside. The Gaels who first gave it its name would not recognise the buildings, but they would instantly recognise the site and the views, though they would wonder at the modern comforts which now exist there. And they would find that Kinminity in its rural setting is still as beautiful as it was, is still a place of human activity and is still loved.

Appendix

Report on Fieldwalking day in Birse on 22nd March 1998

On this day, a party met at Birseside, the former Manse for Birse Church, Birse, near Aboyne, Aberdeenshire, on the invitation of John and Anke Addy, who live at Birseside. The writer, Hugh Cochran, who has a little experience of field walking undertook to organise the day.

The weather - was nearly perfect - Temperature about 7 degrees centigrade, the sky overcast, and no wind.

Aims and objectives - John Addy, who is interested in archaeology, had reason to think that the Birse Church site had been occupied from pre-historic times because of the position in the landscape of the finger of higher ground in the field which hasn't been ploughed yet next to what would have been a bog. It was therefore decided with the consent of the farmer, Neil McConnach of Deerhillock, to do a day's field walking in the field immediately to the north of the Manse as shown on the plan attached. In former times the field will have been a loch or marsh, and for this reason it was decided to walk only round the edges, which are the higher parts of the field.

The Walk - The party met at 11-30 am, and walking started at midday. We walked clockwise starting at the south-east corner, and walked in a band of 30 m wide through sections A to E on the plan. There were 10 walkers, so we were spaced about 3m. apart. Only one of the walkers had previous field walking experience namely Lindsay Stewart

The Finds - The Finds - Most of the finds were 19th Century or early 20th Century broken glass or pottery and most of these were on the south boundary of section A, where there was spillage from a midden within the Manse garden. There were no finds of pottery earlier than 19th Century. However there were two flint finds:

1. A leaf shaped arrowhead measuring 15mm long by 9mm wide. It is of light brown or orange coloured flint and was found by John Addy in section A, row 4 at the point marked on the plan.

2. A sharp two edged knife measuring 46mm long by 14mm wide of grey coloured flint was found by Ian Taylor in section D row 4 at the point marked on the plan.

Drawings **Scale 1:1**

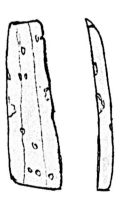

1 The Arrowhead   **2 The Knife**

Conclusions - These two finds are sufficient to justify the day's effort and to confirm the presence, if not the residence, of pre-historic man on that site

Future field walking should be done on the field on the East of Birseside, where there is a ridge of higher ground, and where domestic accommodation is more likely to have been.

Names of those taking part

(a) **Walkers** John Addy, Marie Clarke, Hugh Cochran, Eilidh Scobbie, Donald Silcock, Lindsay Stewart, Anneke Stolte, Ian and Angela Taylor, with Stuart Taylor and Holly Rankine.

(b) **Helpers** Anke and Tom, (lunch) Ben, and Stephen Addy (marking)

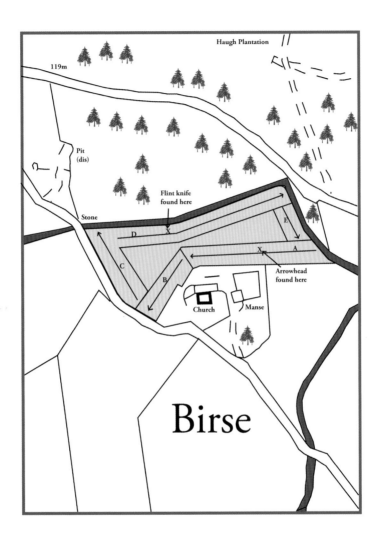

Hugh D. Cochran
Balfour
Aboyne
Aberdeenshire AB34 5DD
26/4/98

References

Aboyne Muniments, National Archives of Scotland Ref GD 181.

Browne, The Right Rev G F (1923) *Echt-Forbes Family Charters 1345 - 1727, Records of the Forest of Birse, Notarial Signs 926-1786* W&R Chambers.

Callander, Robin (2000) *History in Birse*, Birse Community Trust.

Callander, Robin (2003) Report entitled *The Traditional Routes of Birse Parish,* prepared for Birse Community Trust, and held in their archives.

Cochran, Francis James (1840 to 1862) Manuscript notebook entitled *Balfour. Memorandum and Rental Book* containing also other Country Matters, in the custody of the author.

CenturyDictionary (1899) (Nine Volumes of about 800 pages each) The Times, London and The Century Co New York.

Dinnie, Robert (1865) *An Account of the Parish of Birse* Lewis Smith, Aberdeen Republished by Birse Community Trust 1999.

Dinnie, Robert (1882) *Anecdotes of the Late Rev Joseph Smith, Minister of Birse* W&W Lindsay Aberdeen.

Fenton, Alexander (1981) *The Hearth in Scotland* Dundee and Edinburgh.

Fenton, Alexander (2001) *Fires and Firing: an Overview* in The Hearth in Scotland (Ed. Marion Wood) SVBWG , Edinburgh.

Gilbert, John M (1979)   *Hunting and Hunting Reserves in Medieval Scotland.* John Donald

Graham, Henry Grey (1899)   *The Social Life of Scotland in the Eighteenth Century* Republished 1950 Adam and Charles Black, London.

List Of Pollable Persons for the Shire of Aberdeen (1696)   *Vol. 1 Presbytery of Kincardine* reprinted by Aberdeen & North East Scotland Family History Society June 2001.

Macdonald (1899) James,   *Place Names of Western Aberdeenshire* New Spalding Club.

Magnusson, Magnus (2000)   *Scotland: The Story of a Nation.* Harper Collins.

National Archives of Scotland, Register House Edinburgh.

Nicholaisen, WFH (2001)   *Scottish Place-Names* John Donald, Edinburgh.

Records of Aboyne 1230 - 1681 (1894)   (Ed. Charles, XI Marquis of Huntly, Earl of Aboyne, P.C., Ll.d.) New Spalding Club.

Registrum Episcopatus Aberdonensis Vol I & II   *Impressium Edinburgi* MDCCCXLV, Spalding

SMR.   *Sites and Monuments Records,* Woodhill House Aberdeen.

Spottiswood, John (1655)   *History of the Church and State of Scotland.*

Statistical Accounts of Birse Parish, Rev Joseph Smith (1792), Rev George Smith (1842), Rev Robert K Williamson (1950).   Reprint 2001 Birse Community Trust.

Tayler, Alistair and Henrietta (1933)   Editors of *The True and Just Valuatione off the free rent of the whole Shyre of Aberdeen commencing the first day of Jany 1667.* Third Spalding Club MCMXXXIII, Aberdeen.

Wyness, Fenton (1968)   *Royal Valley,* A P Reid, Aberdeen.

Index